SKATE OR DIE

The Last Voyage of the Icemen

STEVEN VIOLETTA

PAGE PUBLISHING
Conneaut Lake, PA

First originally published by Page Publishing 2022

ISBN 978-1-6624-6355-6 (pbk)
ISBN 978-1-6624-6357-0 (hc)
ISBN 978-1-6624-6356-3 (digital)

Printed in the United States of America

To Mom and Dad

With love to my mother and father. You always encouraged me to pursue activities I showed an interest in. But you never pushed me in a direction I didn't want to go, except maybe raking leaves at the cottage.

You both did so much for me growing up. As a child, you passed along your passion for sports, and that created for me lifelong memories and moments. Here are two of my favorites:

> Mom, helping you wash the dishes after dinner while listening to Ernie Harwell and the Tigers games on the radio.

> Dad, you driving me, my midget hockey teammates, and our stinky equipment bags to games all over Michigan.

Love you both so very much. Mom, please read the redacted version of this book.

CONTENTS

PROLOGUE

It was over before it even started.

Before the first skate blade made that crunching noise, cutting into the ice when you push off.

Before the first *clunk* of a hockey stick blade hitting the ice.

Before the first puck went *ding* off a goal post.

After thirty-seven years of Charlestowne Icemen hockey, this would be their last call—one more hockey season. Then it's over. Forever. You'll have to go home because, for sure, you can't stay here.

The end of the Icemen started last September, just over one year ago. It accelerated over the winter and spring. Our landlord, the Charlestowne City government, owns and operates the Olympia Arena through a company called the Olympia Arena Management Company (OAMC). The Olympia Arena is old, failing but still somewhat charming (in a nostalgic way). City Hall and OAMC determined they can make more money from concerts and other flat shows than they can with a losing hockey team that takes up many of the prime Friday and Saturday nights. When that math penciled out, the Icemen were sentenced to death.

Cash talks, and bullshit walks. So let it be written. So let it be done.

City Hall then made two major announcements. The first one was thirteen months ago, last August. The city, OAMC, and key civic leaders announced they would demolish the Olympia Arena and build a brand-new state-of-the-art facility. Construction is well underway as we speak, much of the financing by way of the Government of China. More on that in a second.

7

The second announcement was the nuclear bomb being dropped on the Icemen and their fans. Four months ago, last May, City Hall announced negotiations to include the Icemen in the new arena had failed. City Hall would *not* offer the Icemen a lease agreement to play in the new arena. There was simply too much cash to be had. City Hall and their enablers got greedy. They wanted all the money.

Icemen owner, Rodney Richard Ruthlessberger (Triple R), is no dummy. The public talk a year ago was that City Hall and the Icemen were exploring ways to work together on building a new arena. Privately, Triple R knew better. Quietly, he was desperately trying to sell or move his hockey team to another city. He failed. Several weeks after City Hall declared the Icemen would not be part of the new arena, Triple R finally folded his hand. The Icemen would play one more season and then be dissolved. Go BK.

Like I said, it was over before it even started.

To paraphrase the late great Hunter S. Thompson: The pro sports business is uglier than most things. It is normally perceived as some kind of cruel and shallow money trench through the heart of the entertainment industry, a long plastic hallway where thieves and pimps run free and good men die like dogs, for no good reason.

Who killed the Icemen? There are more fingerprints on that corpse than the back of Madonna's ears. It starts with a long and distinguished cabal of Charlestowne's best business backstabbers, local mafioso, City Hall, and OAMC. There is the Chinese cash, state and US congressmen, some with blood ties to City Hall, and who knew a pork barrel when they saw one. Hell, even the current United States vice president is from Charlestowne.

Over before it even started. Let's start with the usual suspects:

OAMC General Manager Tony Mafasannti—the smiling assassin. Can look you in the eyes, laugh at your joke, and stick a steak knife between your shoulder blades all at the same time. Deep ties to local mafia and state/national politicians. In the pocket of those who wanted the new arena. Worked hard over the last year to sabotage the hockey team's chances of survival.

Mafasannti has relatives in Charlestowne City Hall, Fire and Police Departments. His family owns a construction business that is leading the new arena project.

Mayor Peter Vizzyello—puppet of the Mafasanntis as well as other influential business leaders in the city. (Can't campaign without cash!) He publicly professed to like hockey but wanted to bury the Icemen as much as anyone. His number 1 survival instinct is political—staying mayor—and getting a new arena built with all the construction jobs that goes with it (guarantees his reelection).

OAMC Director of Building Operations Vincent Esposito—biggest prick in the tri-county area. He turns off the arena lights on practicing teams, even if they are still on the ice firing pucks around. They get an hour of ice time, and *on the hour,* those lights go out. When the Icemen are headed out on a road trip, Espo will turn off the ice-making equipment after the second period of the last home game. This speeds up the conversion for moving in a concert or flat show—saves OAMC time and labor. This also results in the melting ice developing puddles in the third period of that last home game.

Espo is never shy about asking the team for a favor like free tickets or player autographs. I've often signed something for Espo, and later that day, it's on eBay. He hates Zamboni driver Donald MacDonald, one of Espo's direct reports. He's jealous of D-Mac and how much the fans love him.

Mafasannti family. The Arena GM employs his relatives throughout Olympia Arena. They have their hands deep into all the revenue streams:

Olympia Arena Lounge. *The* postgame hangout for Icemen players. We drink for free! Managed by Frankie Califano, he sells watches and TVs under the table to players.

He also listens in on their conversations. Frankie relays valuable intel back to the GM, his father-in-law. Frankie married a Mafasannti, Luna. Around here, that is like marrying into the House of Windsor.

Food and beverage. Rocky Mafasannti is in charge. The famous cup-counting scam was his idea—just one example on how OAMC fucked the team for years on revenue.

Beer sales are based on cup volume. Your concession stand starts out the night with five hundred cups. At the end of the night, if only two hundred cups remain, you better have cash on hand for three hundred beers sold. While the game was going on, Rocky and Esposito had the cleaning crew pull old discarded beer cups out of the trash: wash 'em, put 'em back in the rack, and *presto*. Cash for those beers goes in your pocket. This went on for years.

Merchandise Sales. Matteo "Matty" Mafasannti runs this area. Eleven points of sale around Olympia Arena. He sells unlicensed product that never makes it into the official arena inventory manifest. All that cash is siphoned directly to OAMC.

The People's Republic of China. China is financing a big chunk of the new arena construction through the United States EB-5 Immigrant Investor Visa Program.

Created by the Immigration Act of 1990, EB-5 provides a method for foreign investors to become lawful permanent residents of the United States (aka they get a green card). For every nine hundred thousand dollars China invests to finance a business in the United States that will employ at least ten American workers, they receive immigration visas. The Chinese Government is buying their way into work visas and permanent resident status for hundreds of their countrymen.

Uncle Sam, of course, gets a nice commission on each transaction.

And this is how Chinese money financed a new arena in Charlestowne. Last year, through this program, 10,692 EB-5 visas were issued for Chinese nationals.

While that sinks it, let me introduce myself. I'm Victor Barrzini. (My friends call me Vito. You can call me Mr. Barrzini.) I'll be your guide, your Sherpa, throughout this final voyage for the Icemen. I'm the team's player assistant coach, thirty-nine years old, and play like it most nights.

It's my sixteenth season with the Icemen. I was sent down to Charlestowne as a twenty-three-year-old with hopes of getting back to the show one day. I've long since settled for a decent minor league hockey player's salary and the camaraderie of the boys as well as not having to get a real job, like selling insurance or cars.

It's always been about hockey for me—not sure what I will do, could do, away from this game.

CHAPTER 1

Camp, Lee Harvey, and Hog Thursday

First day of training camp
Monday, September 23

This is going to be a fucked-up hockey season. It's got goddamn dumpster fire written all over it already, even before training camp starts!

I pull into the Olympia Arena parking lot to begin the last season of existence for the Charlestowne Icemen. Getting out of the car, I'm flooded with both memories of my previous fifteen years with this organization as well as foreboding thoughts of playing through their thirty-eighth and final season. I'm not going to go into great detail here on *why* it's the final season for the Icemen. That would be picking the fly shit out of the pepper as they like to say in the South. If you read the prologue, all the gory details were in there. The CliffsNotes version:

City hates hockey team.

City manages the building through Olympia Arena Management Company (OAMC).

City decides to implode Olympia Arena and build a new state-of-the-art arena.

City won't negotiate a lease in the new arena for the hockey team.

Hockey team owner fails in efforts to relocate Icemen to another city.

Hockey team owner fails in efforts to sell the Icemen.

Hockey team owner says he'll disband team and fold up franchise at the end of this season.

All aboard for the Icemen's final voyage! Good seats still available.

Guaranteed, there will be plenty of sadness and nostalgia along the way. I just hope there'll be enough happy moments to keep fans from "putting peanut butter on the gun barrel." (PB makes it easier to put the barrel in your mouth. Or so I've been told.)

What's going on inside this thirty-nine-year-old melon of mine as I walk into the Icemen locker room to start training camp? Allow me, please, to quote that first-ballot hall of famer in his own right, Charles Dickens:

> It was the best of times, it was the worst of times, it was the age of wisdom, it was the age of foolishness, it was the epoch of belief, it was the epoch of incredulity, it was the season of Light, it was the season of Darkness, it was the spring of hope, it was the winter of despair.

Wow! Could not have said it better myself. That's why Chuckie D is on the Mount Rushmore of novelists. And I'm an old minor league hockey player who loves it!

Don't worry about me quoting any more Victorian Era writers / social critics. After all, this is hockey. We pride ourselves on being able to use fuck as a noun, verb, and adjective all in the same sentence as in "Hey, fuck you! You fucking fuck!"

Whoa! Don't look now, but there is someone who is going to give us some positive memories this season: Lee Harvey is in the house!

Lee Harvey is my old bud Darren Hightower. We've been Icemen teammates for twelve seasons now, and Darren is loved by everyone: his teammates, the fans, the media, and hockey people.

Even opposing teams have a healthy dose of respect for this man. He's our heart and soul.

I gave Darren the nickname Lee Harvey a decade ago, the season he scored fifty-one goals for the Icemen. He is, as they say in hockey parlance, a sniper. Some people also call him "one" as in one shot, one kill (goal). But the Lee Harvey nickname has stuck. I'm kinda proud of that.

Lee Harvey is a *real* nickname. Too often in hockey, Jonesy or Smitty passes for a nickname. That's horseshit. That's just lazy. Best hockey nickname ever? There was a guy in this league years ago named Don Horachek. His teammates were watching the Jerry Springer Show one day after practice. One of Springer's guests was a married man who got busted by his wife for writing a check to a prostitute for her services. *Whore-a-check.* From that moment on, Donald Horachek answered to Springer.

Back to Lee Harvey. Darren has scored a bushel-basket full of goals every year of his twelve in the American Hockey Association (AHA). No reason to think he won't do it again in this last go-around. He'll likely retire at the end of this season and return to his hometown of Toronto. Maybe coach? Maybe teach? Whatever Darren does, he'll end up in the AHA Hall of Fame. When his thirteenth year is in the record books, Lee Harvey will be in the top five all-time AHA for goals scored, points, and power play goals.

But you know what the best thing is about Darren? He's a complete player, a coach's dream. Fans know him for the booming shot and as an all-star caliber goal scorer. But as his coach and as his teammate, I've loved watching him play hockey at both ends of the ice all these seasons.

As with most prolific goal scorers, Darren isn't going to the HOF for his defensive play. You don't score fifty-one goals in seventy-four games by staying too long in your own zone. But he is a *good* defensive player and is almost always plus in his plus/minus when the season is over.

It's coming out of his own zone, the defensive zone, where the inside hockey guys love Hightower. He's not big but big enough at six feet and two hundred pounds. What Darren *is*, is deceptive. That six-foot frame is mostly legs (which also earned his line the well-deserved tag of the Horsemen. But, sorry, ladies, this is chapter 1, and I'm not going there just yet.) Because of the long legs, Darren doesn't look like he is skating hard. He doesn't have those short, choppy steps a lot of guys need to build up speed. Instead, Darren has these long loping strides as he comes down the right wing with the puck. The opposing defenseman, woefully underestimating Hightower's speed and acceleration, thinks he has him neutralized in the space between himself and the boards. But when Darren gets close, he bangs it into fifth gear. Still not looking like he's skating hard but he is. Darren throws a head fake like he's cutting inside on the D toward center ice. Instead of making that inside move, he actually cuts wide and turns that defenseman.

(How many times have I witnessed this in twelve seasons? A hundred, probably, if not more.) As the defenseman realizes Darren now has a step on him and is going to blow by him on the outside, every one of those one-hundred-plus defensemen suddenly go to their oh-shit face. As in, "Oh shit! I'm beat wide." Once past the D, Lee Harvey takes over, racing down the right-wing Hightower, then fires away. Or fakes the big slapper, gets the goalie to commit, pulls it back, skates a few more strides, and then scores from a different angle. Either way, Bob's your uncle. The red light is on. It's a goal, and it's a thing of beauty.

Here's the best part: The other team knows that's Darren's signature move. They know it's coming sometime during the game. But they still can't stop it—kind of like trying to hit Nolan Ryan's fastball. You know Von Ryan's Express is coming at you over one hundred miles per hour from sixty feet six inches away. But you still can't touch it. That, my friends, is called being physically overmatched. It's a great feeling and the source of a lot chirping when you are the one overmatching people. It sucks when you are the overmatched, and you know it deep down inside.

I wander over and hug Darren. We make small talk about kids, golf games, etc. There is a sense of melancholy hanging in the air. This last season is already weighing on us two veterans. Unspoken between us but right there in our thought bubbles is "I'm too old for this shit."

Third day of training camp
Wednesday, September 25

Days 1 and 2 of training camp were basically physicals, off-ice testing, and equipment fitting. Today, the third day, we actually get on the ice. Head Coach Ken Barnes makes the rounds, welcoming everyone.

Captain Reed Libbet leads us onto the ice, formally starting this last training camp. Libbet is a former NHL player who had some solid if unspectacular years in the Show. He is respected but not feared around the AHA, either physically or talent wise. He's an Alberta kid from the peculiarly named Stony Plain.

Thirty-seven years old now, he'll likely again center our top line with Lee Harvey on his right side and Alfred Slade on the left wing. Teammates call him Pops and Cap (Didn't I tell you that hockey nicknames are usually weak?) Cap is still loyal to the NHL team that drafted him over two decades ago. That organization also happens, at the moment, to be the Icemen's parent NHL affiliate. They have entrusted Reed with helping develop their top prospects. Libbet's key goals this last season: Mentor the kids and don't rock the political boat. Pops has hopes of a front office job with that NHL team after this season is over. In Canada, Libbet is what we call a keener. He'll be the only veteran to dress for all three preseason games so he can give Head Coach Ken Barnes the up close 411 on the other players.

Fourth day of training camp
Thursday, September 26

The Icemen owner finally made an appearance today. Rodney Richard Ruthlessberger (Triple R) stayed for all the morning session, then stuck around afterward to talk to some of the veterans and Coach Barnes. He spoke passionately about the players giving their all this last Icemen season. "Don't leave anything in the tank. Have no regrets when it's all said and done."

I wonder if Triple R feels the same himself. No regrets when it's all said and done. He tried like hell for over a year to move or sell this team—couldn't find a taker. Now he is going to just go BK and call it a day. He looks tired. He's got a little bit of that thousand-yard stare going on, even when he is talking to us. He is as shell-shocked as anyone that this is the last voyage for the Icemen.

It's too bad because Triple R is a very smart person. If he couldn't get this team moved or sold, then it's probably not doable. Once, he figured out a way to claim a tax credit for unsold tickets to Icemen home games. Since visiting teams to Charlestowne came from other states, writing them off as spoiled inventory. His idea was based on some arcane interstate commerce regulation that was probably written in FDR's first term. He argued that once the game was over, that seat was wasted. No way to resell a seat for a game gone by. So he should be able to take the tax credit and write them off as *spoiled* inventory. He also got away with pounding the vino on game nights. Triple R loves his Cabs from the Napa Region, especially fond of the Chimney Rock vineyard. When he's a happy drunk, Triple R will sing the national anthem before Icemen home games. When he's a pissed-off drunk, Triple R has been known to live crash the team radio broadcasts and bitch about the players. That *does not* go over well with anyone, especially the wives and girlfriends listening at home.

Triple R made his money through a lot of varying business relationships. One of his most intriguing is part ownership of the Backcheck Lounge, the preferred watering hole of the Charlestowne Icemen. The Backcheck is not only a bar. It can be a bank! Many payday Fridays over the years, we were instructed, "If you can hold out cashing your check until Monday that would be great. If you need to cash it before Monday, go see Tony at the Backcheck. He'll cash it for you." The Icemen needed the ticket revenue from weekend home games to meet payroll.

On Friday paydays, it was everyone for themselves, a fucking knife fight. Paychecks were distributed immediately after practice.

When word got around the locker room to "go see Tony at the Backcheck if you need money before Monday," it was like the Indy 500 getting out of the Olympia Arena players' lot and over to the Backcheck. Some guys wouldn't even shower, just throw their street clothes on over their practice stink to make sure they were one of the first to see Tony at the Backcheck.

Fifth day of training camp
Friday, September 27

Fifty-four guys in camp vying for twenty roster spots. The reality is only four to five spots are actually open for competition. For most of the fifty-four in camp, this is as close as they will come to The Show.

This number of players banging around is really tough on our trainer, Chuck Hartnett, and equipment manager, Salvatore Lombardozzi. They have been around vets like me and Lee Harvey for around ten-plus years now. They know what we need. We're low maintenance. Majority of the fifty-four are strangers to Chuck and Sal. As the season goes on, the end gets closer, and the price strings will shorten to zero. Sal has already spread the word that the stick room is under lock and key this season. No more wandering in there and grabbing a new stick from your own stash. It might be your pattern, but it's Triple R's cash. You'll have to see Sal or Chuck to get a stick for you. Cost controls.

Most of these strangers have no chance in hell to make this team. Today is the third day of full contact scrimmages, and the strangers are desperately trying to get noticed, maybe dress for a preseason game before they get cut. There are a couple of really good scraps in the afternoon session! One guy that already has everyone's attention is a rookie out of aboriginal Canada.

Todd Hawkes is an Inuit from Nunavut, the newest, largest, and most northerly territory of Canada. (Nunavut separated officially from the Northwest Territories in 1999.) Hawkes was born and raised in Rankin Inlet, the second biggest city in Nunavut at three thousand people. *Three thousand people.* Isolation, destitution, and despair is everyone's relative. It is a bleak existence, a barren wasteland beset with unsolvable social issues like alcoholism, housing shortages, suicide, unemployment, and family violence. Rankin Inlet is not the end of the world, but you can see it from there. If you get a chance to escape from that life, you're going to fight to the death to make it happen.

The story on Hawkes? Family name is Makataimeshekiakiak, which roughly translates from Inuit to English as "black hawk." He changed it to Hawk for assimilation reasons and then altered to Hawkes while growing up. Whether he gets out of Nunavut or dies trying is still a chapter to be written. He likes to drink a lot. And the scouting report is that even when he sobers up a bit during hockey season, Hawkes is always on the edge of falling off the wagon and breaking both ankles. As a teen, Hawkes and his dad used to run the local bars and pick up girls together. As a seventeen-year-old, Hawkes eventually spent six months in the notorious Baffin Correctional Centre after too many drunken bar fights.

The reason Hawkes has everyone's attention in his first pro training camp? If he likes any one thing more than drinking, it's fighting. He's good size at 6'2" and 215 pounds. He's got two things a big-time tough guy needs to be successful: a head that is as hard as granite and a right hand that, if he lands it, will leave your grandkids with bruises. Plus he *likes* it. He embraces fighting. Hawkes has a bit of Bob Probert in him. Probert could hold on and take several of your shots off his coconut while you wear yourself out. Then he'll come back at you hard. Or Hawkes may look to land the haymaker early if you leave an opening. Either way, if he hits you with that sledgehammer right, it's nighty night. Dr. Sleep has just put you to bed.

Hawkes has had one fight so far in camp. It was back on day 1, and he won it. That was against someone about his size. Today, Hawkes caught one of those strangers right on the button with *the right*. Guy was three inches taller and forty pounds heavier, and Hawkes just rag dolled him with *the right*.

There's a lot of demons floating around in Hawkes's head, both personal and professional. He's an indigenous Canadian not only fighting for an NHL job but also fighting for a whole nation of *"undesirables"*. That's a lot to drag around as a rookie in your first pro training camp, especially with the Icemen. We already have a veteran tough guy, Bob Lufthammer, who is bigger than Hawkes. Tougher? That bridge will be crossed one day.

There are a couple of other rookies in camp besides Hawkes. At the other end of the spectrum, 180 degrees and literally worlds apart, is goalie Conner Crosby. Crosby is roughly the same size as Hawkes and also grew up in a small town. But the similarities end abruptly right there. Crosby is an American out of Warroad, Minnesota. After leading his high school to back-to-back state championships, Crosby went on to the University of Minnesota Duluth and won a NCAA Championship in his senior year. He's probably the most anticipated US college hockey goaltender to turn pro since Ed Belfour left the University of North Dakota.

Crosby is the very definition of an entitled WASP: private elementary and middle schools, college-prep-format high school, and full-ride athletic scholarship at a prestigious university. As a result, Conner is book smart. He reads real books like historical biographies and philosophy. The boys have already picked up on his college nicknames like Doc and Professor. Book smart and even hockey smart, yes. But he's street stupid. Crosby is very quiet the first week of camp, both vocally and with his play on the ice. He certainly will make the team, being a high draft pick. But it'd be nice to see him step it up all around.

Annual Maize and Blue intrasquad game
Saturday, September 28

Maize and Blue Game Day. This intrasquad scrimmage marks the halfway point of camp. It's a really good formal competitive scrimmage with fans attending. It's also one last look for the coaches before we start playing other teams in preseason games. I don't dress for this one. It's mostly for the kids trying to make an impression. Coach Barnes wants me next to him on the bench, going to be the last look we get at some of the fifty-four.

I share a pregame meal in the Arena Lounge with Icemen mascot, Stan Cappeletti. His daytime job is an embalmer at his Family's Funeral Home in Charlestowne. It strikes me as we are eating, and I laugh out loud, startling Stan. Last season for the Icemen. The mascot is an embalmer. How appropriate! Dead team walking!

I know Stan a bit from over the years. But halfway through the meal, he goes off on a tangent about how he has already planned his own funeral. Choreographed it, actually, from the music to be played to who he wants to speak. I'm not sure how serious to take him. Stan is a young man, not yet thirty years old. I make a joke about the opening song for his funeral has to be Sir Mix-a-Lot's "Baby Got Back":

> I like big butts and I can not lie
> You other brothers can't deny
> That when a girl walks in with an itty-bitty waist
> And a round thing in your face
> You get sprung, want to pull up tough

Stan is not amused. He moves over to my side of the table and fires up his laptop. He starts to walk me through his masterpiece: *Stan Cappeletti Funeral*.

Song	Artist	Segment	Speaker
Ecstasy of Gold	Morricone/ Rigacci version	entrance music	
Shine On You Crazy Diamond	Pink Floyd	first song upon sitting	
Sound of Silence	Simon & Garfunkel version	second song	*clergy*

Boulevard of Broken Dreams	Green Day	first song after clergy speaks	
Iris	Goo Goo Dolls	second song	
Desperado	Eagles	third song	
The Reason	Hoobastank		*ex-wife*

When the Man Comes Around	Johnny Cash	first song after ex speaks	
Wake Me Up When September Ends	Green Day	second song	
Positively 4ᵗʰ Street	Bob Dylan	third song	*close friend*
Wish You Were Here	Pink Floyd	first song after close friend speaks	
Here I Go Again	White Snake	second song	
The Scientist	Coldplay	third song	*family member*

Heart of the Matter	Eagles (live version)	first song after family member speaks

Don't Look Back in Anger	Oasis	second song	
Keep Me In Your Heart	Warren Zevon	third song	*clergy*

Time of Your Life	Green Day	exit song number 1	
Ecstasy of Gold	Metallica version	exit song number 2	
The End	The Doors		*fini*

I admit to Stan that I'm stunned at the raw emotion, vulnerability, and deep thought he put into choreographing his own future funeral. Confidentially, I'm worried about Stan. Is he contemplating suicide—his last season along with the Icemen? That's all we need is for the mascot to shoot himself at center ice in front of a sold-out crowd.

Stan smiles and says, "I'm fine. Hockey makes me want to live." As he moves back to his side of the table, he adds, "I can put one together for you if you want." I tell him to check back with me at the end of the season! I may need one.

The Maize and Blue intrasquad game itself is nowhere nearly as captivating or enlightening as that pregame dinner with Stan Cappeletti. My head is still spinning. Maize beats Blue 5–2.

There was one player Barnes asked me to just watch him every time he was on the ice. Another rookie, defenseman Damian Steele. Works hard but his game may be a step too slow and a second too late for the AHA. He's definitely on the bubble to make this team, even though he is one of the bigger players on the ice tonight.

As tough as Hawkes is, Steele might match that in being batshit crazy. He wears jersey number 6 because his name is Damian as in *The Omen* movie. Massachusetts kid whose crazy incidents are legend around the hockey world. His teammates back in college called him Triple-6 as in the devil. Or Sybil because of his numerous personalities. It seems Steele tries to pass himself off as an intellect since he went to a division II US college. But that's a bad cover job for him being borderline certifiably nuts. Steele is also an adrenaline freak—skydives, bungee jumps, and races flat track motorcycles.

Steele's chances to make the team improved late in the third period when another defenseman, regular Tommy Pittinger, went down with an injury. Triple-6 actually tweeted almost exactly that after the game. Pittinger has decent talent, a 3-4 defenseman with some upside. But he's not a kid anymore, and the clock is ticking on him proving he can up his game and advance to the next level. Skill is not what's holding him back. It's mental. Pit is part hypochondriac and part real-life fluky injury unlucky. Over the years, he's gone on the DL for injuries like dislocating his shoulder while taking boxed Christmas decorations down off a high shelf.

First preseason game at Old Market
Monday, September 30

Rookie Crosby is going to dress as the backup tonight for the first preseason game. Veteran Norm Zeleski gets the start.

Norm is a bit like Norm from *Cheers*. Everybody loves him and knows his name. (But then the most popular player, especially on sports talk radio, is the backup goalie. Or backup quarterback.) Norm is a rah-rah guy when not playing and working the bench door for the Icemen to change on the fly. Out of nowhere, he'll string together an outburst of rat-tat nonsense to support the boys: "Come on now. Win the draw. Win the draw!" "Let's go here!" "Keep buzzing!" "Good first shift now, boys!"

Hawkes fights one of the Lancers' big young tough guys three times in this game and smokes him badly the last two tilts. Three fights in one game, and you're automatically ejected. As they're going off the ice, Hawkes yells at the guy, "Hey, fuck face! We play you six times during the regular season. You get to fight me eighteen more times this season!" The Lancers' young tough guy did not survive the rest of training camp. He asked to be released the next morning.

Second preseason game at Gotham
Wednesday, October 2

Crosby makes his professional debut tonight on the bright lights of Broadway. He has *not* looked good in camp, getting beat down low-glove side. Gotham's Coach, Dave Haynesworth, asks me about Crosby before the game. No espionage involved, just an old goaltender asking about a young goaltender. Goalies stick together like Samoans in a bar fight. Haynesworth has to be almost sixty-five now. My first year in the AHA, Haynesworth was working in the Metros front office. Long retired but due to some injuries and a call-up, Gotham needed an emergency goaltender. In comes Haynesworth, fifty years old and wearing those old brown leather pads that soaked up water like a paper towel. Haynesworth won the two games he played in. Inspired, the Metros went on to win the Eastern division that year.

Hawkes did not dress tonight. Our veteran tough guy Lufthammer is in. I dress, too, for the first time this preseason, taking a regular shift on defense. Early third period, a young buck comes out to challenge the Hammer. At the face-off, Hammer does a double take looking at the youngster and says loud enough for everyone to hear, "What the fuck, kid? Does your coach know you're out here and gonna get hurt?" Everyone laughs including the linesmen. The young buck is not laughing however. He's shitting his pants. The kid gives Hammer plenty of room on the shift and then sprints to the Gotham bench at the next line change as quick as he can. Haynesworth was not impressed. The kid never sees the ice again. I doubt he'll make it through practice tomorrow without being cut, knowing Haynsie.

This is Hammer's sixth season with Icemen and our fans *love* him. Our home crowd chants, "Hammer. Hammer. Hammer," in a slow melodic way when they want Barnes to send Hammer into the game to settle shit down when the other team starts running the Icemen. Our music guy plays MC Hammer's "Can't Touch This" after he wins a fight at home. Crowd goes bonkers. Bob is definitely a fourth-line guy if not the tenth forward most nights. He can't skate a lick, he's a real bender, but he's as tough as they come. It will be interesting to see if we carry both Hammer and Hawkes. If nothing else, it would impact how much forward I play versus falling back to play D.

Uneventful game. Crosby struggles, and he loses 6–1. Barnes almost pulled Crosby after a bad goal to open the third period. He looked down the bench at me, and I shook my head. Nah, leave him in there. Haynesworth asked about him. There must be something for Haynsie to take an interest. His nickname has been Yoda for years. "Pass on what you have learned." The old goalie just wants to impart some wisdom to the great white hope.

Eleventh day of training camp
Thursday, October 3

Today is Hog Thursday. It's an annual Icemen training camp event, a tradition that goes back even before my time. On the second Thursday of camp, after practice, the boys all head to the Backcheck Lounge. The Backcheck promotes it as just another ladies' night with drink specials. Few know that it's really the annual Hog Thursday.

Most of the guys are in for Hog Thursday. Some of the married ones even! The premise is each player puts one hundred dollars into a pool, and whichever player hustles the fattest, ugliest girl *and* fucks her wins the pot. That last requirement was added several years ago. It *must* be a clam slammer to win. Back in the day, all you had to do was pick up the fattest, ugliest girl to win. You didn't have to plow her. Trouble was some of the vets recruited fat, ugly girls to show up at the Backcheck on Hog Thursday. If that player won, he'd split the pot with his ringer.

Even if you don't win the pot, most guys do okay on Hog Thursday and get their love muscle massaged. A handy is not unusual. Even a blow job on the hood of a car in the parking lot.

At thirty-nine, I happily put my Benjamin in the pot but really don't try to win anymore. In my younger days, maybe twelve years ago, I won Hog Thursday in back-to-back seasons! Two in a row. And it's true: Defending the belt and winning two in a row is a lot harder than winning that first time.

Third preseason game home against Old Market
Saturday, October 5

Third and final preseason game, our first one at home. Icemen don't play a lot of preseason home because it's a bad draw for ticket sales. And we don't want the added expense of staffing a game night event. Road preseason games are always easy bus trips to the teams closest to you.

A home game means we'll see J. F. LeGault smoking away. LeGault grew up on dairy farm in Sainte Foy, Quebec, not far from Quebec City. Quebec produces about 40 percent of Canada's annual dairy needs. The LeGault farm cranked out lots of milk, but they were known all over Canada for their fromunda cheese.

But it's not cheese that puts the "go" in LeGault. This Quebecois loves his cigarettes pregame, between periods, and postgame. He's told me that he even smokes in church! Olympia Arena is owned and operated by the City of Charlestowne. There is no smoking in any city facility.

The Icemen had to build a phone booth outside our dressing room in the hallway for LeGault to smoke on game nights. The city hates this and is always sabotaging his phone booth so he can't light up in there.

LeGault can smoke a pack every game night as far as I'm concerned. Despite his darting, he has the best speed of all our defensemen. Also, he has very strong offensive skills, and he runs our number 1 power play unit.

I don't dress tonight, but a lot of regulars do. So does Steele, on the bubble and playing his third straight preseason game. Steele reminds me of the Tasmanian devil. While Hightower skates effortlessly and deceivingly fast, Steele is the opposite. His skates are going a million miles an hour, but he looks like he's barely moving up the ice.

I sit with our scouts high in a corner section of the arena. Some fans recognize me and wander over to say hello. You can tell it's a preseason game. Most season ticket holders have given tonight's tickets to friends or family. The ushers are getting lots of questions from people who don't come to Olympia Arena much. They're asking where their seats are. Where is the closest bathroom?

Everyone I talk to tonight has a sense of sadness about this final season. It hangs around their necks like a truck tire on a chain.

CHAPTER 2

Opening Night, The Code, and Evil Roy

Monday, October 7
Five days until opening night

Training camp has now pretty much run its course. We are down from fifty-four players to twenty-two, and Barnes likes that. Fairly detached from coaching in camp, Barnes is more of an observer and talent analyst when you have fifty-four players to look at. He'll step up his interaction with the team now as we are only five days from puck drop. The last opening night puck drop for the Charlestowne Icemen.

Barnes is my friend and boss. This will be my fourth season as his assistant coach/player. Barnes is an extremely hard worker and a former NHLer who didn't play long enough or good enough to make the NHL big money. He had a couple of brothers who were also decent NHL players. Since his playing days, Barnes has worked his way up through the organization: first, as a scout, then assistant coach, and finally, head coach. He needs to work. There are no retirement ponderings for Barnes, not when you are twice divorced with child-support payments.

Barnes is a good coach, though, and his players respect him. He is also known for two things throughout the hockey world: He was the last active NHL player to *not* wear a helmet. (Barnes always got by on his toughness and the softness of some of these modern players baffles him.) His propensity to use movie quotes to inspire his players. (Barnes critics like to point out that he has few original thoughts when it comes to motivation. And that is likely related to being the *last guy to not wear a helmet in the NHL.*)

I'm sitting with Barnes in the early afternoon after practice. While we are talking player personnel, the Icemen general manager, Rudy M. Lakor, pops into the coach's office. The next words out of his mouth are simply the first team-altering utterance of this final season, "Get measured for rings, boys. I just won you the Koontz Cup."

Now Lakor is your typical minor league hockey GM—part talent scout, part snake oil salesmen, and part idiot savant. He's swung some big trades over the years for the Icemen. And he's known throughout the AHA as a master schedule maker. The Icemen always end up heavy on home games the second half of the season. That's great if you are battling for playoff position. Sucks if you are out of the race and home games have zero importance to the fans.

As much as Lakor has his GM life shipshape, his personal life is the Titanic. About three years ago, he started having an affair with an Icemen's front office employee and got her pregnant. Next thing Lakor knew, his wife had put him on irrevocable waivers. And he's shacked up with this twenty-five-year-old Icemen employee, living together on his houseboat. Lakor's kids are barely younger than dad's new girlfriend. They disown him and cling to Mom.

But today, Lakor is at his GM best. He has orchestrated the acquisition needed to fuel a playoff run. Lakor has picked up Duncan Craigsen.

Snake oil, anyone? How many gallons should I put you down for?

Barnes and I are confused and very concerned. Craigsen has a well-earned reputation as a locker room cancer. A former high first-round draft pick in the NHL, the future was bright for Craigsen six years ago. Even when he first got sent down to the minors, Craigsen had a one-way contract. So he was playing in the minors and making NHL money. His teammates back then tagged him with nicknames like Dunkie Rich and Cake Boss.

Craigsen is now on a two-way contract. In the NHL, you can make serious coin. In the minors, you make shit. He's drank and played himself deeper and deeper into the minors. He has gone from making millions of dollars a season in the NHL to the AHA minimum of thousands. Now in Charlestowne, he'll be sulking more than Hitler did in the spring of 1945. Wouldn't surprise me if Craigsen even built a metaphorical bunker and refused to come out.

This is a former NHL first-round pick. Craigsen obviously has the tools. The problem is he doesn't always bring the toolbox to work. He just went through training camp with Springfield over in the AHA Western division and certainly could help them. Then why is he here?

Suddenly, the light bulb goes on above my head. Lakor and Springfield coach, Hank Moody, are good friends. Moody and their NHL affiliate don't want Craigsen around poisoning his team's chemistry. Exile him to Charlestowne where Moody's buddy Rudy will be happy to take him.

Lakor leaves. Barnes and I discuss how to spin this as a positive to the Icemen. Someone will lose a roster spot to add Craigsen. It turns out to be popular veteran, Art Woodhouse. That won't sit well with the boys. They love Woodhouse, especially his cooking. Barnes and I agree. Craigsen is probably best to center the second line and be a regular on special teams.

Tuesday, October 8
Four days until opening night

Four days until the regular season opener. Good time for me to introduce you to a monthly segment for your reading entertainment: *Icemen hockey insider lesson of the month*. This month's lesson: *The Code*.

The Code is an unwritten set of rules that allows hockey players to regulate and control physical play themselves. Self-policing on fighting. You learn The Code growing up and playing hockey. If you claim there is no code or no one understands what the code is today, you never played hockey at a level where you needed to worry about The Code because you sucked!

In 1866, the Marquis of Queensberry penned twelve rules that form the basis of modern boxing. He gave it the very uncreative title of *The Marquis of Queensberry Rules*. But at least he wrote the damn rules down.

So the Q has twelve written rules for fighting. Fight Club, as you'll recall, has eight unwritten rules. I'm going to say Fight Club really has only seven unwritten rules because rule number 1 and number 2 are both "You don't talk about Fight Club." Tyler Durden created those rules. Tyler Durden. What a fucking *great* hockey name by the way. Tyler Durden. Gotta be a rugged defenseman.

We don't know who originated The Code for the hockey world. Regardless, the code has seven rules. And you're right. It's about fucking time someone wrote them down! You're welcome.

(1) Heavyweights only fight heavyweights. If you are not a heavyweight, then stay in your weight class. Never fight down, fight someone smaller than you.

(2) Exception to rule one: If you run the other team's superstar, you can expect payback from their tough guy. Maybe not in the game you are currently playing. Maybe not next month when you play these guys again. Maybe not even until next season. But rest assured, you will need to eventually pay the piper. And the piper could come in any size.

(3) No sucker punches. Or jumping a guy from behind.

(4) Shift change. Never fight the other guy at the end of his shift, especially when you are early in your shift. He's tired and you're not—unfair.

(5) Never take unfair advantage, like an opponent stepping on a glove or stick and falling to ice.

(6) When to stop throwing hands. When the other guy hits the ice, the fight is over, even if you have a punch cocked, loaded, and ready to fire. Pull it back if he's on the ice.

(7) Rematch. You *always* owe the other guy a rematch if you beat him—always.

Coming up. November's *Icemen hockey insider lesson of the month*: hierarchy on the hockey bus.

Wednesday, October 9
Three days until opening night

Old number 5 is back in the Maize and Blue. Defenseman Pat Bradberry is a steady defensive-minded backliner. He probably leads our second set of defensemen as the number 3 or number 4 D.

He is an Ontario guy going 5'11" and 190 pounds. Pat has been a reliable, if unspectacular, AHA player for the past seven seasons. His teammates love him, especially the goalies who are often the beneficiaries of his work. But if vanilla was a player and not a flavor, it would be Pat Bradberry. The bald head does not help him when it comes to personality.

Don't get me wrong. Pat is one of the most popular guys in the room. While his game on the ice is modern, his wardrobe off the ice is definitely stuck in the 1970s. Whether Pat is coming to Olympia Arena for a home game or traveling for a road game, he always wears a suit that is a shade of brown—always. This has earned him more nicknames than one man deserves. He's been tagged as the Baron of Brown, Boss of Beige, King of Khaki, Tycoon of Tan, Admiral of Amber, Bishop of Bronze, Governor of Gold, Prince of Peach, and more.

The boys sometimes wager on what color suit he'll wear to the rink for home games. The pool has already started for the home opener on Saturday. Bishop of Bronze has the early lead.

On a serious note, I've heard secondhand talk that Pat's marriage was in trouble. Too bad. He was a good husband, not a cheater.

Thursday, October 10
Two days until opening night

Four rookies have made the Icemen roster. As far as potentially having a long successful NHL career, voted most likely is a nineteen-year Russian superstar.

Alexei Badinoff is blessed with it all. He's big at 6'2" and 210 pounds. He's got Hollywood movie star good looks. He's got all the tools: can skate, shoot, pass, and play physical. He is a stone-cold killer on the power play. He even kills penalties pretty well for a teenager. All the same skills that his hero has, three-time Stanley Cup champ, Alex Ovechkin. Badinoff even wears Ovie's number 8.

Like many Russians, Badinoff pretends *not* to understand English. He understands when he has to, like when his agent is talking free agency. Alexei is guarded about opening up. He grew up in the bleak, isolated Oblast region of Russia where it's literally dog-eat-dog. Hockey there was and still is the Russian version of playing your way out of the hood. And now his first worldly life experience is as a teenager in this quirky American city with a team in its last season. I can't tell yet, but I think the final voyage of the Icemen is more amusing to him than sad.

The boys have already started calling Badinoff Boris. While grabbing his crotch, Alexei replies under his breath in broken English, "I've got your moose and squirrel right here." Some of the boys also call him Bad Enough. Regardless of nickname, Alexei has way too much raw talent to be in the AHA for more than one season—two at the absolute most. He's what us career minor leaguers call a remember when. Remember when Boris played here? Enjoy it, fans, as he blazes through Charlestowne like a meteor. Boris will be an NHL star in a couple of years and never pass this way again.

Friday, October 11
One day until opening night

Final practice before game day. This is the last time we'll go really hard before tomorrow's opener. On game days, like most teams, we do a forty-five-minute skate in the morning—light on pucks—stretch it out, then home for a pregame nap!

We are sitting down with Barnes after practice today to set the eighteen we'll dress for the home opener. Based on practice this week, it looks like we'll be going with this:

Goalies	Zeleski
	Crosby

Defense Pairings	LeGault/Steele
	Pittinger/Bradberry
	Hogaboom/Richatelli

Forward Lines	Slade/Libbet/Hightower
	Badinoff/Craigsen/Karvaala
	Budler/Chrisler/Hawkes
	Lufthammer

Saturday, October 12
Home opener versus Wilson Falls
Win 6–1

After pregame skate this morning, I grab a coffee with one of the few Olympia Arena employees I respect and like: Zamboni driver Donald MacDonald or as everyone calls him, The Dude. He looks just like Jeffrey Lebowski from the beard and haircut right down to the bowling shirt. A lot of people who call him the Dude have no idea what's his real name.

He reminds me of a guy named Herbie Redmond from my Detroit days. Herbie was the dancing groundskeeper from the 1970s and 1980s Tigers baseball teams. He pumped up those Tigers fans and got them roaring when the grounds crew dragged the infield. D-Mac does the same thing with Icemen fans, especially those in Section 8. When Lebowski comes out on his Zamboni, he is standing and dancing to the music, many times the soundtrack from *The Big Lebowski*. Among his signature moves are a handstand on the steering wheel and also spinning around in the seat, driving the Zamboni backward.

We talk about life after the Icemen. It's not promising for either of us. Donnie Mac doesn't think the Olympia Arena Management Company (OAMC) will bring him with them to the new building. His boss, director of arena operations, Vincent Esposito, hates him. Espo is jealous of all the love Donnie gets. Espo forgets he's the Dude, man!

We are back in the Icemen locker room after the pregame warm-up. It is twenty minutes until we drop the puck for keeps. As part of his pregame chalk talk, Barnes delivers the following quote from Marine four-star general, James Mattis: *The most important six inches on the battlefield is between your ears.*

In other words, *play smart.* The boys respond to that. Hightower bags two in a big win, including one of his patented oh-shit moves. Veteran Zeleski got the start and the win. But we all expect that goalie pecking order to flip eventually—just a matter of when.

It was a physical game for a while. Then we pulled away, and Wilson Falls went to sleep. They wanted no piece of Hawkes or Hammer. Let alone Damian Steele who ran around all night with his hair on fire. Triple-6 didn't see a lot of ice time but was certainly given a *lot* of room when he was on.

The best part of a 6–1 home win: The crowd gets *free french fries*! As part of our Bumpa's Burgers sponsorship, "Anytime the Icemen score six or more goals and WIN, you win." You will get a free small fry when you redeem your ticket stub. The franchisees closest to the arena hate this promotion. They get pounded with ticket stubs and people wanting free fries right after the game, which is usually fifteen to thirty minutes before they close. That fryer is already cleaned. Fuck!

If a cocktail is more your postgame desire than free fries, welcome to the Olympia Arena Lounge located on the main level near gate two. The Arena Lounge manager is Frankie Califano. His ties to City Hall and the Charlestowne underworld are deep. Frankie is pouring the drinks and playing all the angles. He sells watches and TVs under the table to players and fans he knows are regulars (But they're not hot!) Frankie sips on a rum and Coke he keeps under the bar while managing the postgame activities. Next to the rum and

Coke is a short-barrel Mossberg twelve gauge with pistol grip and loaded with five rounds just in case. Frankie calls it his organizer because if need be, it will very quickly organize the room.

Players drink for free in the Arena Lounge after games and so do the better-looking puck bunnies. We appreciate it. As one former Icemen said many years ago, "If hell had an open bar, I'd shake Satan's hand."

Frankie listens in on the player conversations and relays info back to the coaches and the owner's son, Baron Richard Ruthlessberger aka B R-squared. Or the info could go to Olympia Arena general manager, Tony Mafasannti. It depends on who Frankie can score the most points with. As they like to say in Texas, Frankie is so crooked, he could swallow a nail and shit out a corkscrew. But Frankie is connected. He married a Mafasannti girl, Luna.

Sunday, October 13
Home versus North Jersey
Lose 3–2 in overtime

Crosby plays well in his first regular season start as a pro. But he's outdueled by the veteran, Bobby Ennet. Lyle Akouree gets game winner in OT on a sweet tip right in front of the kid. That Akouree fucker is pretty good.

Line of the night. Slade said to Wild Bill Hunter of North Jersey who was running his mouth nonstop, "Shut the fuck up. If I need any lip out of you, I'll rattle my zipper."

Monday, October 14
Bus to Gotham for a Tuesday game. We leave after 2:00 p.m. so the owner doesn't have to include lunch in the player per diem. It's like a ten-hour bus ride even with lead foot Randy Beacon driving. That puts us into the hotel well after midnight. All to save about two hundred dollars in lunch per diem. Is this how it's going to be all year? Yeah, probably. Cost controls.

I sit next to Slade for the long ride and a chance to catch up. We pound several cold ones. Just a couple of American kids living the dream.

Alfred (Al) Slade is our two-way stud. At 6'2" and 185 pounds, he can play at both offense and defense ends of the ice. Slade goes into corners and usually comes out with the puck. He blocks shots and back-checks ferociously. He doesn't look for trouble on the ice. He'll leave that to heavyweights, Hawkes and Hammer. But Slade can handle himself just fine with the gloves off, and the other players in the league know it. He gets his space, especially when Slade sets up in front of net on power play, screening the opposing goalie.

Slade plays on the horsemen line with Hightower and Libbet. They are not called the horsemen for their speed and horsepower. But it is only chapter 2, and I'm *still not* going there. In the meantime, ladies, let your imaginations run wild.

Al grew up in the Saint Paul, Minnesota, suburb of North Oaks. Quite a different place from where I grew up in Detroit City. But he's no suburban Sally. How did we get the name Evil Roy? A few years ago, Slade was driving hard to the net from left wing. Hightower had the puck coming down the right side and fired at shot. The goalie kicked it away but right onto Slade's stick who was only three feet away now. Slade one-timed that rebound and tucked it hard right up under the crossbar. Puck hit the water bottle, which went straight up in the air. Al slams on the brakes and throws snow all over the goaltender. He then catches the water bottle midair and takes a long swig off it, the whole time staring down the goalie. Slade downs the damn water bottle, flips the empty at the goalie's feet, and skates away. No opposing player said a word, let alone get pissed off enough to do anything about it. Slade just prison fucked your goalie and then wiped his dick on the rest of your faces. And you did *nothing*. The Evil Roy legend was born.

Evil Roy and I also have a running gag for, what, over six years now. When one of us catches the other daydreaming or looking a bit down, when you make eye contact, you ask him, "You okay?" The standard answer is "No. But I'm working on it."

Tuesday, October 15 at Gotham
Lose 5–2

Whenever we make the trip to the big city, I always think about Metros head coach, Dave Haynesworth, and I smile. Dave is an AHA Living Legend with a capital L, first as a player and now as a coach.

Haynsie was young when he made the move into coaching, maybe thirty-five years old. He was playing in Elmdale, then suddenly retired and went behind the bench about halfway through that season. It's *very* difficult to coach guys who you played with, even tougher when its guys you played with just yesterday. So Haynesworth had his work cut out for him in Elmdale, coaching a veteran-laden team that was out of the playoff race and didn't give a shit. The vets also thought they could get away with murder because their old goalie and drinking buddy was behind the bench.

On a cold, windy February night that first coaching season, Haynsie decides he's had enough bullshit. The Elmos are on the road and out on the town the night before a road game. Haynesworth had given the team a midnight curfew at practice that day, but he knew only the youngsters on the team where likely to abide by that. Haynsie goes down to the hotel lobby about 11:30 p.m. and starts to chat up the cute female night manager. To Haynsworth's delight, she turns out to be a hockey fan.

Haynesworth says, "You're a hockey fan? I'm the head coach of Elmdale. Did you know we are staying in your hotel tonight?"

The manager says, "Yes, of course, I did."

Haynesworth says, "Would you like some autographs?"

The manager says, "Of course. I would love that."

Haynesworth says, "Okay, stay right there. I'll be back."

Haynesworth goes back to his room to retrieve a hockey stick. He's back down at the desk by 11:55 p.m. and tells the night manager, "Here you go. Get your autographs on this!" She's pumped.

As the Elmdale players stumble in well after the midnight curfew, they're only too happy to autograph a hockey stick for this cutie. About 6:00 a.m., Haynesworth rolls back down to the front desk and tells the night manager, "I need to borrow that stick for a couple of hours. I promise I'll bring it right back."

Haynsie did bring that stick back to the night manager. After, he held it up at the pregame skate that morning with the team gathered around him and loudly announced, "Okay. The following players are fined five hundred dollars for missing curfew last night."

That's just one of several classic Haynesworth stories. Maybe the next time into Gotham, I'll tell you the one where he got his own team fined over a pregame ceremony on his own home ice. I'm reminded of that one because of what happened tonight before our game with the Metros. It's Gotham's home opener, so like most hockey teams, they plan a rather elaborate pregame ceremony featuring showstoppers like pyro, smoke, flash pods, live bands, etc.

The Metros had all that and more programmed leading up to the introduction of their new mascot who has been patiently waiting inside the Zamboni ice bin. Stashed inside a relatively closed space while the Zamboni idled, I should add. While the pyro and lasers are going off and the live band is playing, the mascot is slowly getting fumigated by the Zamboni exhaust.

It's now time for the mascot's grand entrance. The Zamboni carrying him drives out to center ice to a massive ovation. The Zamboni stops at center and gradually raises its ice bin. The door on the ice bin flops open as designed. Not by design, however, the new mascot slides out of the bin and hits the ice face-first. Motionless, he lays there for several awkward seconds until the arena staff realizes he is out cold. Knockout by Zamboni exhaust! You can't make this shit up.

Wednesday, October 16

Day 3 on the road trip. A strange story is circulating at practice this morning about that crazy fuck, Steele. No one is sure if the story is true or if someone is fucking around with us. Steele posted on Facebook this morning about a close friend dying suddenly. We should have paid more attention at that point.

Regardless, here is how the rumor goes. Apparently, Steele's dog died Monday the fourteenth, about a half hour before our bus was scheduled to leave for Gotham. Steele can't get ahold of any neighbors. His girlfriend is not picking up his calls. To avoid being late for the bus, Steele does the only thing he can think of. He wraps his Australian cattle dog, Dundee, in tin foil. Then puts Dundee in his freezer until he gets off the road trip and can deal with the situation properly.

We are afraid to ask Steele about the authenticity of dead-dog-in-the-freezer rumors. Slade steals a line from his favorite author of all time, gonzo journalist, Hunter S. Thompson: "Some may never live, but the crazy never die."

Friday, October 18 at North Jersey
Lose 7–4

Start of a long road trip: four games in six days. I'm in my sixteenth season now with the Icemen, and *every year,* this part of October we pack up and hit the road so Olympia Arena can host the North American International Auto Show.

Trip did not start well in North Jersey tonight. We shit the bed to be honest about it. The House Painters are stacked and can play the game anyway you want: skate, grind, and fight. They intimidated us physically and humiliated us skill wise. The 7–4 final was not that close.

One thing (two, I guess) they have that we don't are the Barbour twins. Bill and Bobby buried us tonight. Their line had a hand in all seven of their goals, and Bill scored three. When you watch the Barbours work their magic together, you can't help but think of the Sedin twins in Vancouver years ago. Bill and Bobby have that twin intuition going to start with. When you factor in how long they have been playing on the same line together, since peewee hockey, well, that's a chess game you are going to lose almost every time. The Barbour twins are always at least one step ahead of you. Their distracters call them Thelma and Louise. They're not the most physical players in the league. I know one thing: They can play on my team anytime.

The twins were a whole city block ahead of Pittinger tonight. The Bradberry-Pittinger pairing drew the Barbours most shifts, and

Pitt got exposed badly. He was minus four! And this is Pitt when he's healthy. Tommy has some talent, a 3-4 defenseman with upside. His issue is staying healthy. The boys call him Whirlpool or D. L. Pittinger is a bit of a hypochondriac and has missed some games over the years because of general soreness. But he's also suffered some real-life fluky injuries. The clock is ticking on Pitt to up his game and move up to a higher competition level.

One of my favorite game responsibilities when I'm not dressing and working behind the bench: calling out for a change on defense. When I want the Bradberry-Pittinger duo to go out onto the ice, I get to yell out the change as "Brad Pitt. You're up." Damn, I'm easily amused.

Saturday, October 19 at Old Market
Lose 2–1

I forgot how much I hate playing here. They call it *Old* Market for a very good reason. *Everything* here is as fucking old as dirt. Their Barn has to be fifty years old. What a shithole! Their arena workers look like they were here the day the building opened. Even the colors of the walls and seats are that shit-brown and avocado-green earth-tone colors that were so popular in the 1970s. It's like stepping back five decades when you play here.

And then there is Lancers' goalie, Elmer Hackareinin, who stoned us tonight. That old fucker is so fucking old, his social security number is 002. The Dead Sea was just sick when that old Findlander was born.

Old Market also has the toughest fans in the AHA. They boo Santa Claus for Christ's sake. Few years ago, a Lancers fan sitting behind the visitor penalty box was banging on the glass too hard, and it fell into the box. The visiting player in the box was startled. The Old Market fan looked at the visiting player, now without a one and a half inch piece of plexiglass between them, and decided what the fuck. He jumped down into the box, fought the visiting team player, and held his own!

We did play better tonight but still lost 2–1. Big Saturday night out in Old Town for the boys' postgame. They get our radio broadcaster / VP communications, Don DeMarko, to come out and pound shots with them.

Sunday, October 20

Early wake-up call, 5:00 a.m., for a bus to Tri-Cities for Monday game. Select bars in Old Town don't close until 4:00 a.m., so I know some of the boys never went to sleep—plenty of time for that on the nine-and-a-half-hour bus ride to Tri-Cities.

Maybe an hour down the road, we stop at a McDonald's to get some breakfast to go. Many of the Icemen stay sleeping. DeMarko is sick from the night before and thinks some eggs might settle his stomach. He's horribly mistaken. Shortly after we get back on the road and he's fired down two Egg McMuffins, DeMarko's world turns upside down. At least his stomach does. We've all been there, some of us more times than we'd like to admit. You've crossed the Rubicon, and there is no turning back. You are going to puke and puke hard. DeMarko, being the devious bastard he is, sizes up the situation quickly. There is no way he's going to ask Beacon to pull the bus over. Running the gauntlet of prone, sleeping hockey players between himself and the bus toilet is not a viable option. DeMarko pulls the head fake and pukes into his empty McDonald's bag. He puts it inside his backpack before sliding and hiding the whole thing under his seat.

DeMarko might have gotten away with that at least until the next stop when he could toss the McDonald's bag properly. The problem is DeMarko is sitting in one of those bus seats that has a floor heater underneath to keep the feet of the people in that general area warm. The heater eventually melts a hole in the backpack. Not long after, a burning nylon smell begins to waft through the bus that heater hits the McDonald's bag. It's like setting off pepper spray in a confined space. People's eyes are watering. When the smell of cooked vomit gets around, some of the other riders begin to puke as well.

Bus driver Beacon then makes an emergency turn off on the side of the highway. It takes close to an hour to clear the bus of puke stench.

The players are pissed. Barnes is *really* pissed. I don't feel sorry at all for DeMarko, though, because he is a grade-A first-ballot hall-of-fame asshole.

He's been the voice of the Icemen for twenty-plus years now. Outside some of the players, he's probably the most public face of the organization. DeMarko has been very methodical to construct his public brand as a loyal, family-oriented, and churchgoing person who is just happy to be doing the same thing year after year. The truth is he hates his life and his wife.

He hates even more the sober reality that he can't get a broadcasting gig with an NHL team. On the road, DeMarko is a party animal and a pig. He usually rooms with Trainer Chuck Hartnett on the road. Chuck is always at the rink, so Don has the hotel room to himself almost always.

Once in Cleveland the night before we played the Steamers, the NBA Cavaliers were playing. DeMarko goes to the Cavs game with a young hottie intern who works for the hockey team. She has keys to the Steamers' offices. So DeMarko ends up fucking her in the Steamers' boardroom during the Cavs game. When telling the story, DeMarko loves to emphasis how he could hear the crowd chanting and cheering on the Cavs while he's pounding away. "Those cheers were for me!"

It doesn't stop with road booty. DeMarko makes a game out of putting a word somewhere in his broadcast, a unique word that his squeeze is listening in to hear it, and she knows it's for her. He'll tell her to listen to the game broadcast, and "I'll work in a word just for you because I'm always thinking about you." It has to be a ten-dollar word that no one uses in normal conversation—something like ubiquitous or ambrosial. It's the audio equivalent for puck bunnies that Carol Burnett did for her kids, tugging on her left ear at the end of each TV show to signal her kids good night.

Monday, October 21 at Tri-Cities
Lose 3–0

Long bus ride. Long ugly road loss. Daniel Fumay shuts us out 3–0. We made him look like the second coming of Patrick Roy. Every shot we took was right at him. Even Hightower kept shooting the puck right into his chest.

Closest we came to a goal was early third period. Libbet rips a shot high to Fumay's glove side, but it hits the pipe and deflects out of play.

Fumay says, "Nice one. Almost had me."

Libbet says, "Yeah, smoked the pipe, just like your mom, the champion pipe smoker."

Even the linesmen lost their shit laughing. It took extra long to line up for the face-off.

Tuesday, October 22

Bus to Musktown. I decide to spend time with Da "Dale" Budler, one of the few bright spots from last night's loss in Tri-Cities. Budler battled all night long, even took a double-minor slashing penalty with less than a minute to go in the game. Dale had apparently had enough of Lincoln Ford's bullshit (aka the missing link).

Ford has no idea what destruction he likely dodged. I knew a bit about Budler before this trip, including his toughness and absolutely no hesitance to give you a good two-handed chop across your wrist if required. He is not a huge man, but at 5'10" and 180 pounds, he is pound for pound one of the tougher guys around the AHA. But until I sat across the aisle from him on the bus to Musktown, I had no idea he had killed some of his own countrymen.

Dale is thirty-two years old but only in his fourth season in the AHA. His pro hockey career was delayed a couple of years by serving in the Czech Republic Air Force. He worked his way up to colonel and picked up two great nicknames: Buzz and Red Baron. Buzz fits his hockey playing style perfectly. He buzzes around like a hornet and takes the other team off their games—gets in their heads. We call that a shit disturber. Opponents get so worried about swatting Budler, they forget to play their own game and often get whistled for the retaliatory penalty. Budler usually draws the opponent's number 1 or number 2 line and is our best face-off winner.

Eventually, our bus talk turns to his time in the Czech Air Force. I find out he flew more than twenty combat missions in the short-lived Czech-Slovakia conflict from six years ago. Czech regions of South Moravia, Zlin, and Muravia declared their independence and tried to reunite with Slovakia with whom they share a common border. Budler flew a JAS 39 Gripen fighter/bomber then and in those twenty-plus sorties dropped all kinds of bombs on the breakaway states.

Budler and I had been having a couple of beers on the bus, and suddenly, the tone turned very somber with his Air Force stories. I asked if bombing his own countrymen bothered him. Budler said no. He spoke of the detachment and surrealism of killing people from a height of twelve thousand feet and how its nothing like what Army ground troops go through. Air Force bombing is "very similar to playing video games."

Budler tells me about conversations he has had with his United States counterparts, particularly pilots who fly B-2 bombers. The B-2s are based at Whiteman AFB outside Kansas City. With one aerial refueling, the B-2 can fly from KC, drop a bomb load in the Middle East, and be back in KC in under thirty hours. Talk about surreal. Those pilots tell stories about flying out of Whiteman, bombing Iran, then getting back to Kansas City in time to pick up pizza for the kids on the drive home.

That reminds me of the old *Doonesbury* comic strip from the Vietnam Era. North Vietnam man was standing in a rice paddy, shaking his fist at the sky. US bombers have just destroyed his village from fifteen thousand feet above.

North Vietnam farmer says, "How can you do this? There are woman and children in this village. We have no fight with you! How do you sleep at night?"

USAF pilot, flying away, says, "Hey, did you hear the Yankees won two last night?"

Copilot says, "This might be their year."

Wednesday, October 23 at Musktown
Lose 4–2

Hawkes did not dress. We found out at the morning skate he got smoked in a bar fight the night before—after curfew, possible concussion. We know he is a big-time drinker. Are the wheels coming off his season already? I guess Hawkes misses his bar fight wingman—his dad!

Hawkes was out, so Lufthammer dresses instead. In the second period, Hammer fights the Generals' goon, Matt Wilsen. They trade a couple of punches and then Hammer hits Wilsen square on the snot locker with an overhand right. All of a sudden, Wilsen is leaking oil faster than the Exxon Valdez. All the way to the Generals' bench, he leaves a bright-red trail about three inches wide. As Wilsen heads in for repairs and Hammer heads to the sin bin, Steele says to Wilsen, "Hey, fuck head. Thanks for donating blood. Keep playing hockey." Then Steele laughs hysterically—very creepy.

Hammer and Hawkes have two contrasting fighting styles, and it works for each of them. Hammer is an over/under guy. He'll work the jab, the hook, and then try and catch you with an uppercut. Hammer prefers his right hand but can knock you out with the left too. Hawkes is all about that H-bomb of a right hand. Hence, the nickname One Punch. What Hawkes has, though, that many don't is super stamina. He can wait you out, let you get tired from banging your fists on that granite head of his, and then he'll launch the right when your defenses are weakened.

Thursday, October 24

It turns out, the Steele dead-dog-in-the-freezer story is *not* urban legend. It's 100 percent true. This was verified by multiple players' wives and girlfriends. Steele's girl invited some guests to watch the Saturday, October 19, AHA game of the week broadcast featuring the Icemen at Old Market. The party was at Steele's apartment.

When Triple-6's girl went to put some food in the freezer before the crowd arrived, she found Dundee.

Friday, October 25
Home versus Texas
Lose 8–1

Never in this one. You can probably guess that from the score. Crosby gets chased early second period after giving up five goals on eleven shots. As he gets to our bench, the Marshalls' Derek Dean drops this nugget on the kid, "Hey, tampon! Guess you're only good for one period after all." I see Steele staring at Dean, making a mental note. Dean better be ready next time we see them. He could end up wrapped in tin foil and frozen too.

Zeleski finished out the game. Our home crowd does the first Hammer-Hammer-Hammer chant of the season. But Barnes keeps Hammer's ass nailed to the bench in this rout.

Saturday, October 26 at Wilson Falls
Win 6–4

We've lost seven in a row and haven't won since opening night for fuck's sake! After getting crushed at home last night 8–1, its panic time in C-Towne. Icemen owner, Triple R, and GM Lakor decide to call a team meeting before the bus leaves for Wilson Falls. Air it all out. What the hell is the problem? Is it because it's our last season? Is it because we just suck? *What the fuck is going on?*

Polite small talk is exchanged. Players are trying to be upbeat and make a couple of constructive suggestions to the owner. Then Duncan Craigsen, who hasn't said shit in two weeks about anything, raises his hand and drops this bomb.

Craigsen says, "I honestly think one of the reasons we've struggled is because of the shitters here in the locker room. The stalls are too narrow. It feels claustrophobic to sit in there and dump."

The owner, stammering and not sure what to say, says, "I'm confident those stalls are up to code. It's a city-owned building, and they would have to maintain at least the minimum code for stall width to pass inspection."

Craigsen says, "Well, I'll tell you what, Mr. Ruthlessberger. If you're so confident, come on down here next week sometime and pinch one off with me. We'll compare notes."

The boys don't know whether to laugh or go blind. Lakor just glares at Craigsen, drilling holes into him with a death stare. But Lakor has no one to blame but himself. Craigsen is here because Lakor took him off Springfield's hands as a favor to his butt buddy over there, Hank Moody.

The bus to Wilson Falls after the team meeting is raucous. The boys are incredulous at Craigsen. Badinoff just keeps shaking his head from side to side, even when no one is talking to him. I end up talking to Craigsen about other very important things, like who is the GOAT (greatest of all time) rock drummer? The Canadian guys, especially Ontario, all vote for Neil Peart of Rush. I concur and declare Peart the greatest of all time.

Perhaps inspired by Craigsen (he wants to think so), we win 6–4, snapping that seven-game losing streak. Maybe we can turn this around.

Sunday, October 27

We show up for practice today and half of the glass on LeGault's smoking booth is missing. The arena tells him a driver moving cars during the North American International Auto Show backed into it, taking out one side. He asks for more details. He gets none. They just liked to fuck with Frenchie.

Monday, October 28
Home versus Cleveland
Lose 6–4

Or maybe we are not going to turn this thing around! This is now officially the new low point of the early season. We lose a stinker

6–4, an ENG by the Steamers Reggie Dunlapp putting the final nail in the coffin.

But the big story was what happened with our fans in Section 8. Section 8 is the die-hard of the die-hard Icemen fans. Their two goals at an Icemen game are to cheer on the home team verbally and visually annihilate the visiting team. These are that fans that taunted Peninsula goalie, Albert MacKartnee, in his first game back after a thirty-day rehab for coke addiction. He didn't play but dressed and was on the visitor's bench. Section 8 sits right behind the visitor's bench. To welcome Ballwagger back our fans in the first three rows behind the bench, all waved clear plastic bags filled with a white powder.

Then there was the time Tech City came to town. Their star forward, Marc Mayhew, was dating movie star Kaley Cuoco at the time. A couple of dozen Section 8 fans came to game with large posters of Kaley. They made rude gestures at the posters with bananas, dildos, eggplants, etc.

After losing seven of eight games and now down at home to despised division rival Cleveland, Section 8 riots. They've had enough. They've put out hard-earned money to buy season tickets for this last voyage with the Icemen, and right now, they are on the Titanic. Man the life boats. After the Steamers' fourth goal early in the second puts them on top by three, Section 8 goes Captain Bligh on the team—*mutiny*! Section 8 gets up en masse and walks up the stairs to the concourse. Now remember our bench is *across* the ice from the visitors. So when Section 8 gets up to leave, we can see the whole maneuver right in front of us.

We shoot each other looks up and down the bench. All the players saw it. How can you miss an entire section of two hundred fans getting up at once? We all figure Section 8 is headed home or down to the Arena Lounge to start postgame drinking early.

Suddenly, those two hundred fans from Section 8 are right behind us. They had disappeared from view, walked 180 degrees around the concourse, and resurfaced behind our home bench. Section 8 cares little for the fans already sitting there. Pushing and shoving breaks out as the Section 8 fans muscle their way down behind our bench.

They start to pound on the glass and scream obscenities at Coach Barnes. They are shaking the glass so violently, it begins to move in the stanchions. Arena security and the limited Charlestowne City PD on assignment are as caught off guard as anyone. The officials stop the game midplay until this settles down. Thankfully, clearer heads prevail. Some of the Section 8 fans return to their own seats behind the visitor's bench. Others call it a night and head to the Arena Lounge and the Backcheck to drink. I wouldn't go near either place postgame tonight. Section 8 has revolted and they're itching for a fight.

That scared us straight. We rally from the 4–1 deficit, but it was not enough. A day late and a dollar short. We leave right after the game for Musktown. Very quiet bus ride. We are embarrassed. I've never seen Barnes so despondent. Lots of sleeping on the bus. No one was playing cards or video games. The lights are all off. Every player is deep in thought and questioning themselves.

Tuesday, October 29 at Musktown
Win 6–3

We managed to pull one out tonight—a win we desperately needed. If you think there is no such thing as a must-win game in October, well, you have not been paying attention.

Halfway through the game, it looked like more same old same old. We were losing 3–2 and getting outplayed. Then Gerry Hogaboom lowers the boom on Tim Parker with a huge open ice check. Just like that, we have new energy and go on to win 6–3. The Generals never score another goal after Hogaboom went boomtown on Parker. Parker is out of it as he is being helped off the ice. As he passes Slade, Evil Roy says, "Sweet dreams, Parkie. Welcome to boomtown!"

Keeb Chrisler scores the game-winning goal. Lufthammer and Richatelli chip in with goals too.

Wednesday, October 30

Inspiring himself with that big hit and an assist on Chrisler's GWG, Hogaboom pulls off his first practical joke of the season. He's the team prankster. If someone has fucked with your stuff, you can bet the Big Swede was in on it. You can always tell when he strikes no matter what part of the locker room you're in. When someone screams, "Fuck! Boomer! For fuck's sakes," you know he has violated someone. This time, it's a timeless classic hockey prank: baby powder in the hair dryers.

Badinoff goes to blow-dry his magnificent head of lettuce, and as soon he hits on, the hair dryer shoots out enough white baby powder to cover his face and shoulders. Boris looks like the Joker before he applies red lipstick and green eye shadow. To add insult to injury, Hogaboom often tapes these pranks and posts them on Twitter and his YouTube channel. He has lots of followers especially back in Sweden.

Hogaboom is a big 6'3" 220 pound of a man. He's our most-physical defenseman. The Big Swede plays with an edge. He's got grit, like playing against someone wearing a sandpaper jersey. If he knows he can physically intimidate you with the potential of a big hit, you're likely to take less trips through the neutral zone looking backward for one of your D to headman the puck to you. Boomer has some offensive skill and usually runs the second power play unit. Not the hardest shot from the point you'll see but he can really sift a shot through traffic and creates a lot of tip chances. Hogey is really known for changing the tempo of a game by stepping up and catching opposing players with their heads down. Call it lowering the boom, kaboomed, or catching the boomtown express. If you are on the receiving end of a Hogaboom teeth rattling hit, there is no shame in counting your Chiclets afterward.

After practice, I notice Mr. Hockey spending some time with Crosby. Looks like Mr. Hockey is working on the kid's mechanics.

Thursday, October 31
Home versus Elmdale
Lose 5–3

It is Halloween costume contest tonight! All kids in costume get free candy on the way in. The arena hates this, cuts into candy and salty snack sales.

I hardly ever complain about the officiating, but the refs sucked donkey balls tonight. We gave up three power play goals on five chances. Four of those five penalties called against us were wildly questionable. Two of the Elmos' three PPG were by their star, Mike Santoze. We didn't play well, but refs didn't give us a chance to get back into it. Too many penalties equal too much energy used to kill penalties equals no continuity to our game. Coach Barnes is still reeling from the Section 8 riot three days ago. He loses his shit early third period after we got called for a ticky-tacky minor interference penalty far away from the play.

Barnes says, "Hey, Zebra! That whistle isn't a dick. Get it out of your mouth."

Ref says, "Go fuck yourself. Enjoy the rest of the game from the dressing room."

Although we lose 5–3, there is one bright spot: The Icemen wins best costume contest for impersonating a hockey team that actually gives a shit.

Our October record is 3-8-1. That's last place in the Eastern division, kids. Fuck me.

CHAPTER 3

A Death in Dallas, Bus Hierarchy, and Yes-vember

Friday, November 1

It was great to see Keeb Chrisler get the game-winning goal last Tuesday at Musktown. He's not known for his offense, so when the Elf chips in with a goal here and there, that's huge. He played his best game of the season so far and would have been the number 1 star if this was a home game. Those fuckers in Musktown give no quarter. They don't ask for any either, even with three stars.

Chrisler is one of those guys who just goes out and does his job night in and night out—a bunch of dirty work that doesn't show up on the stat sheet at the end of the evening. Elf leads the first penalty kill unit and centers the checking line. He's matches up against the other guys' top two centers all night. Keeb is one of the smaller Icemen at 5'9" and 170 pounds. But he's a great face-off man, one of the AHA's best. He also sees time on the second power play unit. He's got good hands.

Chrisler is a farm boy out of Saskatoon, which is the biggest city in Saskatchewan. But at three-hundred-thousand population only the seventeenth largest city in Canada. The Canadian Western boys (British Columbia and Alberta) and our guys from Ontario love to make fun of Chrisler and Saskatoon. When the Elf starts talking about doing something or going somewhere, one of the boys will invariably ask, "How you gonna get there, Keeb?" To which another Icemen always retorts, "Why don't you take the noon balloon from Saskatoon?"

Saturday, November 2
Home versus Tri-Cities
Lose 5–4

Zeleski plays the first in back-to-back home games. Late in the first period, Z-man takes a high hard one right off the melon. He's stunned and lays there for thirty seconds without moving and his eyes closed. When he finally gets up, T-Bird captain, Brant Frewson, skates over and lightly taps Zeleski on the pads. "Good thing that shot hit you in the head," says Frewson. "Won't do any damage there."

The real entertainment for the home crowd tonight is provided by the Olympia Arena PA announcer. Charlestowne fans and especially the Section 8s, have always made fun of Tri-Cities and their players as hillbillies. Like us, the Thunderbirds are made up mostly of Canadians, a half dozen or so Americans, and the rest Europeans. Our fans treat every Tri-Cities player as if they're from Locust Ridge, Tennessee, or Butcher Hollow, Kentucky. Tonight, our PA announcer takes it to another level.

Apparently, no one knows our PA announcer is going to go completely off the rails. Maybe he wants to get fired. I hope so because he is canned immediately after the game by the Olympia Arena Management Company. It was fun while it lasted. He gets off these zingers and has the fans LLOL (literally laughing out loud). "Attention, please, hockey fans. There is a tractor in the parking lot with its lights on. A tractor with its lights on. Tennessee license plate E-I-E-I-O. Team doctor to the Tri-Cities locker room, please. Team doctor to the Tri-Cities locker room. Team Doctor Billy Bob Joe Ray Jerry Lee Clampett to the Tri-Cities locker room. A reminder, fans, that Olympia Arena is a smoke-free facility. And for our guests here today from Tri-Cities, that includes corn cob pipes."

Good shit! But the T-Birds has the last word. I can almost hear the chant coming from eastern Tennessee, "Scoreboard, fuck face!"

Sunday, November 3
Home versus Texas
Win 4–1

Two home games on consecutive nights, so Crosby gets tonight's start. The Professor is up to the test stopping thirty-seven of thirty-eight shots. Crosby stands on his head and makes several spectacular saves on the Marshalls. I can't put my finger on it. But since Crosby sat down and talked to Mr. Hockey last Wednesday, he looks like a whole new goalie out there, not only more confidence but has a different technique.

Steele plays better tonight and finally catches up with Texas tough guy, Derek Dean, early in the third period. Double D has been in Steele's gunsights since the October massacre, Friday the twenty-fifth, and Texas shellacs us at home 8–1. Dean does some trash talking when Crosby gets pulled early. Steele has made a mental note of that.

Dean knows he was going to have to dance with Steele, but the two aren't on the ice at the same time very much tonight. Early in the third with Dean out there, we change up the D, and Steele goes right up to him.

Steele says, "Answer me true or false."

Dean says, "Huh?"

Steele says, "It's simple, asshole. True or false. I like my teeth."

Before Dean can say huh again, the gloves are off. They each land a couple of inconsequential punches, and it looks like the linesmen are going to jump in. But then Steele switches hands and feeds Dean a left hook that takes him down. Dean hits the ice—fight over. Steele skates to the penalty box and on the way, looks at Crosby and gives him a big old wink. The boys like this. I got your six.

Spirits are good after the win. I tell the team, "Great win. Nice way to stand up for each other, Steele in particular. Listen up. Tomorrow's practice time is ten to twelve. Ten to twelve."

Monday, November 4

We all know Hawkes is not the sharpest knife in the drawer. He'll never get mistaken for Einstein's half-wit cousin, let alone Einstein.

When I told the team after the game last night that today's practice time would be ten to twelve, Hawkes interprets that as meaning practice starts at 11:50 a.m. He shows up a little after 11:00 a.m. as you normally would for an 11:50 a.m. practice time. Problem is practice has already been going on for over an hour since 10:00 a.m. This is bad, particularly in the light of the after-curfew bar fight that kept Hawkes out of the October 23 game in Musktown.

Hey, Hawkes, let me translate for you. Ten to twelve means 10:00 a.m. to noon, you stupid fuck.

I'm beyond pissed. Words fail me, so I do the Pontius Pilate: wash my hands of the whole thing. Barnes will have to deal with Hawkes on this one.

The boys are on Hawkes after practice.

Slade says, "You're as dumb as a fucking shrub."

Libbet says, "You couldn't spell cat if I spotted you the C and the T."

Zeleski says, "I bet you are capable of tripping over a wireless network."

Hightower says, "I heard you went to the library looking for Facebook."

Tuesday, November 5

Bus to Tech City—the start of two games in three nights on the road. Then back home for a Saturday game with Musk. Three games in four nights. This is a good early test to see how real we are.

I sit across from Richatelli on the bus. Not only is Tony an American but he's a townie! A local kid! Tony was born and raised in Charlestowne and spent his childhood in and around the Olympia Arena, idolizing the Icemen of a generation ago. His family has deep community ties including a sports bar that is the PG-13 alternative to the hangouts like the Arena Club and Backcheck Lounge. The Richatelli's bar is more postgame for families with young kids and groups of teenagers. More pizza and Pepsi there than Patron and Pussy at the other two places!

Townie is a stay-at-home D, which is why he usually is paired with Hogaboom. That allows the Big Swede to jump up into the play and try and nail someone with a check, knowing Townie is back and covering up. Tony, though, is overcautious at times with the puck. Barnes and I have both worked with him on taking a calculated risk once in a while. He has decent speed and should be able to get up ice more often to create an odd man rush. Tony married a local girl last year. I can see him taking over the family sports bar one day.

Okay, kids, while we have some more window time on the bus to Tech City, let's do another.

Icemen hockey insider lesson of the month. This month's lesson: *hierarchy on the hockey bus.*

Now I've been playing hockey for thirty-five years from peewee travel to now sixteen years as an Icemen. The hierarchy of who sits where on the hockey bus *never changes*. Like The Code, bus hierarchy is unwritten and strictly enforced. God forbid, it's your first time on the bus, and someone from the Icemen has not told you where it is appropriate for you to sit.

The bus is the workhorse of minor league hockey. Few teams fly anywhere. It's too expensive. A ten-to-twelve-hour bus ride to play a game is not unusual in the AHA. The typical charter bus has fourteen rows, four seats per row with an aisle down the middle, so a 2/2 setup for each of the fourteen rows.

That gives us fifty-six seats. The typical hockey traveling party is anywhere from twenty-four to twenty-six people. It depends on how long the road trip is and if any injured guys may not play. You can't be caught short a player and dress only seventeen!

Normal Traveling Party

| game night lineup | 18 | spare player(s) | 1 | coaches | 2 |
| radio broadcaster | 1 | equipment manager | 1 | trainer | 1 |

And here is the bus hierarchy. Don't *dare* sit in the wrong section. No one sits behind the head coach unless you have a reason to speak with him, like the trainer updating him on injuries. But after you have spoken to the coach, you *must* go back to your normal seat.

Row	Bus Driver	Door
1	Assistant Coach	Head Coach
2	Broadcaster	OPEN
3	Equipment Guy	Trainer
4	OPEN	OPEN
5	Rookie	Rookie
6	Rookie	Rookie
7	Goalie	Goalie
8	Quiet Veteran (reader)	Quiet Veteran (reader)
9	OPEN	OPEN
10	Beer Drinkers	Beer Drinkers
11	Beer Drinkers	Beer Drinkers
12	Veteran Player	Veteran Player
13	Senior Veteran (Poker)	Senior Veteran (Poker)
14	Senior Veteran (Poker)	Senior Veteran (Poker)

Passing time on the bus

You can only drink so much beer, play so many video games, and lose so much money at cards before a hockey player needs something else to do on the bus. A popular game to pass the time is called *One Day, One Month, One Year.*

There are only a couple of rules.

Eligibility. Any female is eligible to nominate: dead, alive, fictional, friend, family, and (especially) coworker. The only prerequisite is the female you put forward *must* be someone the other players know of. Anna Kendrick, Scarlett Johansson, Wonder Woman, booster club President Lynda Robinson, Richatelli's sister Amy, and the blond with huge tits in sales are all acceptable.

Term. Once you've put forward your female, present your case for why you want *One Day, One Month, or One Year* to bang her. The other players around the table then get to agree or disagree with you and defend why they'd like to fuck that woman *One Day, One Month, or One Year.*

Factors. Defending your choice of who you would like to fuck for *One Day, One Month, or One Year is* complicated. There are numerous factors, of course, and that is multiplied by the perversion and depravity of those around the table. Someone's *One Year* is another's *One Day.* That's one reason it's such a great game.

Here is a sample guide based solely on my preferences, patience capability, and penis. You may or may not agree. Either way, get ready to defend your position.

One day. There is no doubt this experience would be mind-blowing, the best sex of your life. You would be seriously drained and ruined for life with future women. The quality of this sex not only rocks your world, it would change it forever, like that big-assed meteor that killed the dinosaurs.

Your one-day choice then is *incredibly* hot and sexy. But her shrill voice, her political views, her insanity, or her ability to kick your ass means you could only handle one glorious day of sex with her before she drives you crazy. There is no way mentally you would make it through a month of sex with her before you wanted to kill her in her sleep. Think Sarah Palin, Angelina Jolie (Lara Croft), Amy Winehouse, very early Jane Fonda (Barbarella), Ronda Rousey, Gal Gadot, Britney Spears (from 2001), Harley Quinn, Halle Barry, Lois Griffin, Kristen Stewart, Casey Anthony, Gwen Stefani, and 1995 Fran Drescher.

One month. Just like above, mind-blowing life-changing sex. *Plus* you could have adult conversations with her (if you want). She's able to talk intelligently about sports, cigars, cars, music, etc. The four pillars of life. But after a month in which you covered all sixty-four positions of the Kama Sutra, you've run out of things to talk about. And it's time to move on.

Think First Lady Kimberly Guilfoyle (sorry, President Donald Trump Jr.), Danielle Colby (*American Pickers*), Lana Kane (*Archer* TV show), Danica Patrick, Dana Perino, Princess Leia, Richatelli's sister Amy, former Florida Attorney General Pam Bondi, porn star Nina Hartley (1980s version), Scully from *The X-Files*, Rashida Jones, Brie Larson, Ainsley Seiger, Mariska Hargitay (*Law and Order*), Chanel West Coast, and Lily the brunette from the AT&T commercial.

One year. One whole year. We're making a real commitment here. No off-ramp for 365 days. Assume the sex will be epic, life-altering. The conversation will be intriguing and profound. *And* now we require a touch of that girl-next-door wholesomeness but with a healthy helping of dirty-girl mentality. To sum it up: a wife at the neighborhood barbecue but a whore in your bedroom. You may want her to meet Mom (eventually), but you wouldn't trust her on a girl's weekend in Vegas.

This is rarified air and requires a unique skill set to be nominated for one year.

Think Kaley Cuoco, Chris Evert (1970s), Meg Ryan (1980s), Jessica Alba, Betty Cooper (*Archie* Comic Books), Maria Sharapova, Kate Mara, Cindy Morgan (*Caddyshack* & *TRON*), Amy Adams, Cobie Smulders, Zooey Deschanel, Detective Kate Beckett (*Castle* TV show), Kate Beckinsale, Jennifer Anniston, and Detroit's own Kristen Bell. (Huntington Woods technically. She's Woodward Avenue between Ten and Eleven Mile. I was Woodward Avenue between Seven and Eight Mile. Kristen makes my list!)

Coming up. December's *Icemen hockey insider lesson of the month*: navigating the booster club class system.

Wednesday, November 6 at Tech City
Win 4–0

Crosby is spectacular. He not only notches his first shutout as a pro, but it is also a road shutout. That's a huge pick-me-up for this team.

The Professor's talk with Mr. Hockey is paying off. We know Mr. Hockey could beat goalies like a rented mule. He is, after all, one of the all-time great NHL goal scorers, a hall of famer. Little did we know he is also a goalie whisperer. That's why he's Mr. Hockey I guess.

Barnes is Christmas Eve excited after the game. While throwing around attaboys and good on yas, he veers off course. A 2–1 start this month, and Barnes changes the name to *Yes*-vember. "No-vember? No-vember? Fuck no! The hell with no. This is now officially Yes-vember! As in, *yes,* we care, and, *yes,* we can win fucking hockey games!" The boys let out a cheer. A road shutout and cold beer helped with the enthusiasm.

Friday, November 8 at Springfield
Lose 2–0

We are on the other end of the goose egg tonight. Dick "Doc" Weston pitches the shutout for Springy. Bright spot: Crosby again plays really well, just got outdueled on the road by a quality AHA veteran. LeGault has a rare night where he struggles. The Spirits Erik Hapkey notices.

Hapkey says, "What's a matter, Smokey? Didn't you have a ciggie before the game? A Pepsi? Poutine. Come on, froggy. You suck tonight."

LeGault says (muttering under his breath and acknowledging he's off tonight), "Tabernac!"

Saturday, November 9
Home versus Musktown
Lose 4–2

Cub Scout Night. This is a huge group ticket sale for the Icemen organization. Two thousand scouts here: Boy, Girl, Cub, Rover Scouts, Brownies, and Girl Guides. All are welcome as long as you buy that seventeen-dollar group ticket! The players enjoy this promotion. With so many kids at the game, the energy level in the arena is much higher than usual.

While we are talking high, Nestlé sponsors Scout Night. Any scout in uniform gets a free king-size Crunch bar. Some genius in the Icemen marketing department also thought this would be a great night for a plastic bugle giveaway. "We're blowing our horn about our new condo complex," says a dangling tag from each bugle. Ticket department had scheduled this night for scouts. Marketing (through political pressure) went and scheduled plastic bugles sponsored by Mafasannti Developers, which also happens to be partners with City Hall on the new arena. Tickets didn't know what marketing was up to and vice versa—classic no communication.

I really can't blame marketing. Turns out our owner was trying to play nice in the sandbox with the city way back when there was still a chance Icemen would move into the new arena. Owner agreed to let this city partner, Mafasannti Developers, do a promotional giveaway on a Saturday night in November (Yes-vember). And that's how you get chocolate candy bars and plastic bugles given to scouts on the same night.

The noise these kids make on their bugles after getting wired on chocolate is great for game atmosphere. The ride home in the car with Mom and Dad, however, is not so great. Parents were lighting up the Icemen switchboard immediately after the game, asking to speak to "the obviously childless moron who gave out bugles and candy bars on the same night."

Monday, November 11

We are attending the booster club meeting later tonight. We can't wait (said no player ever). I'm sure many of them will still be bitching about chocolate bars, bugles, and losing their hearing on the postgame drive home.

President of the Icemen Booster Club is Lynda Robinson, a former puck bunny who is now too old to get into the player's pants but still hot enough to sleep with the owner's son (B R-squared) and Charlestowne Mayor Vizzyello. In separate relationships, I assume! Over the past summer, Lynda was the backdoor (pun intended) communication between ownership and the mayor when the public talk was on how to save the Icemen. Mayor gave it lip service for a while and went through the motions. Mayor never wanted to include the Icemen in the new arena planning. But he did enjoy tagging Lynda.

Tuesday, November 12

Bus to Peninsula for a quick one-game trip. I start out sitting in row two, right behind Barnes, so we can go over possible line changes. Captain Libbet is sitting in row one behind the bussie, talking to Beacon. When I'm done with Barnes, I drift back to row three and find myself sitting across from Sal, our equipment guy. He's intently reading the National Enquirer. Headline says, "WWII Bomber found on moon." I say, "Wow. Think we're building a Space Force base up there?" Sal does not answer me.

While I was sitting behind Barnes, Libbet and bus driver, Beacon, were having a loud conversation. I couldn't help but hear some of it. Beacon is a sales guy for the local car dealer who is also an Icemen sponsor, DePasto Oldsmobile. Beacon talks to Cap about how much "they are going to enjoy Dallas road trip later this month." Sounds like a group of clients/VIPs are traveling with ownership to Dallas for the Marshalls game. I make a mental note to tell Barnes later. He hates surprises like that, especially if ownership is going to be at a road game.

Wednesday, November 13 at Peninsula
Lose 6–5 in overtime

We pick up a road point with this loss in OT so we should be happy. But it feels like a real loss. It is a clusterfuck of a game. We blow the lead three different times. Zeleski deserves a better fate. He plays pretty well, which is a strange thing to say in a game where you give up six goals. But we leave him hanging all night. Mark Bono scores the GWG in OT on a scramble in front of Zeleski. It seems like the puck sits there for two minutes, and no Icemen could clear it.

There is some ugliness too. The commissioner is likely to get involved. Hawkes dresses and has to go through a barrage of racial insults all night from the Panthers' Bob Slydell. I know Bob very well. We played juniors together back in Detroit. Our families back there are close.

I see Bob a lot in the off-season around Detroit. We were even teammates on the Icemen for a period a couple of years ago. But tonight, I see a side of Bob Slydell I have never seen before. For some reason, Slydell decides to chirp at Hawkes all night long, but it isn't the usual hockey trolling. It is deeply personal stuff about his Inuit background. In fact, it is an insult to everyone and has no place in society, let alone a hockey game.

Each time Slydell is on the ice with Hawkes, he would bait him and call him derogatory names: pie face, harpoon chucker, Eskihomo, whale blower, and Klondike fag bar.

During my first time on the ice, when I hear it, I go right over to Slydell at the whistle, not to fight him but as a friend. I say, "Maybe you don't know this kid's rep. But, Bobby, trust me. You better not wake him up." No impact. Slydell keeps going. Lucky for him, it is a close game, and Hawkes doesn't want to take a penalty, maybe cost us the game. Then in overtime, neither guy hit the ice. But you know Hawkes makes a mental note to straighten out Slydell the next time we play Peninsula. Quick check of the schedule says that is about two weeks away, December 4 in our barn.

Thursday, November 14

Getting ready for practice, Pittinger injures his back tightening his skate laces. He pulls a back muscle while pulling the laces tight! He's out for the weekend. That means I'll likely play D Friday against Springfield and Sunday at Michigan.

Detroit is my hometown, so I'm glad to be in the lineup for a return to the old stomping grounds. It's always exciting to play in front of family and friends. But I'm not excited about drawing the short straw and matching up against Springy's Hapkey and Akouree from Michigan in consecutive games. They are young studs and *very* skilled. And I'm too old for this shit.

Friday, November 15
Home versus Springfield
Lose 3–1

I see something tonight I have never before in thirty-five years of playing hockey. Game is delayed for over an hour in second period. A fan crawls out over the ice and onto some arena roof structure, then freezes, locks up, and couldn't back up! I was told later there are some holes in the original Olympia Arena walls in the upper bowl. These are made a few years to rerun some TV and Internet cable. The holes are not very big. A normal-size guy couldn't wiggle through there. But this skinny guy is curious (translation: drunk). He crawls through the hole and slithers out on an I-beam 100 feet above the ice to get a selfie—just a little something for his Twitter fans.

When he looks down and realizes where he is, and a fall would certainly be fatal, he freezes. The Charlestowne Fire and Rescue team has to come in to get him down. Hockey officials cancel the last 3:11 of second period and tack it onto the start of third period.

Tonight is our fourth loss in a row, and the boys are starting to lose their shit. In a postgame interview with local TV, Hammer snaps and almost punches out the reporter. Local TV is almost never here for postgame. Local stations come in and shoot the first period, maybe part of the second. Hopefully, they get a couple of goals to use on the 11:00 p.m. news.

The postgame scrum surrounding Hammer is comprised of the usual suspects: Icemen beat reporter, visiting team beat reporter, DeMarko and visiting radio guy are all doing their postgame. Hammer is sitting in front of his locker naked, except for a towel over his lower half. He's quietly answering questions from the usual suspects. The local TV reporter, who looks like he is twelve years old, decides to get involved. I'm sitting straight across the room from Hammer so I've got ringside for the whole thing. The TV reporter looks at his cameraman and tells him to turn on the camera-mounted light. He's gonna jump into the scrum with a couple of questions.

As soon as the light goes on, Hammer immediately spins his head around to his left and says menacingly, "Turn that fucking light off!" Stunned, the cameraman clicks off the light. Hammer resumes talking to the usual suspects. The kid TV reporter (intern) waits a minute or two. Then he nods at the cameraman to hit the light again. He's not leaving without getting his questions answered. The light goes on. This time, Hammer bolts up off his chair and squares around, towering over the cameraman and kid reporter. The towel hits the floor. Hammer is fully naked, all 6'4" and 235 pounds of him, muscles taut as a snare drum, veins starting to pop out of his forehead. "I said," Hammer utters through clenched tooth sneer, "TURN OFF THAT FUCKING LIGHT."

The TV reporter gets it this time—light off and packs up and out the door. No postgame interviews tonight.

So much for Yes-vember. Back to No-vember after four straight losses. Let's get on the road and see if some bonding time will help. DeMarko loves the road. He'll get laid. Sal runs with him sometimes. They call each other Ripken as in they turn a double play on some chick.

Sunday, November 16

We are getting on the bus to Detroit right now. We will play the Michigan Command on Sunday. I feel like sitting by myself at least for the first several hours. Tons on my mind besides four straight losses and our lack of consistency. With a game at Michigan comes friends and family to deal with. Plus a lot of Detroit memories always come flooding back, some good, some bad. I stare out the window and watch the Midwest roll by.

I am Detroit born and raised—not the fucking suburbs, not fucking Bloomfield Hills or Farmington or Novi (bonus points if you know how Novi got its name), and for sure, not one of the fucking pretentious Grosse Pointes. My hood was Woodward Avenue and Eight Mile, Little Street called Keating—really close to the old State Fairgrounds. (Novi is no. VI or number 6. Sixth stagecoach stop out of Detroit back in the day.)

I was big for my age playing youth hockey. As a midget (fifteen-year-old), I was already 5'10" and 177 pounds. Add another two inches on skate blades, and not too many opponents wanted to fuck with me. I played the tough-guy role pretty well. Back in those days, I had a big curly black afro and black sport glasses with tape on the nosepiece. I looked like a cross between former Cleveland Indian Oscar Gamble and one of the hockey Hanson Brothers. Pro hockey was an eye-opener. Not only are the players on the other team just as big (or bigger) than me now, they are more skilled. And a few are even tougher.

It didn't hurt to look tough in 1970s / early 1980s Detroit. I wasn't born when the July 1967 riots set the near west side of Detroit on fire for five days. But growing up there, years later, it was still evident that 1967 remained an open sore on the city's soul. When you have a riot that the local PD, Michigan State Police, and Michigan National Guard can't put down—and you need five thousand troops from the US Army's 82nd and 101st Airborne Divisions to get control—that, my friends, is a major league riot. The Army actually occupied Detroit for over a week. My parents showed me pictures of Army paratroopers manning sandbagged and heavily armed checkpoints on major street intersections. All the Detroit police precincts were fortified and protected by the US Army.

The official count from the five days of riots in July 1967 were forty-three killed and seven thousand arrested. The killed number is likely higher. Urban legend around the city is that DPD were dumping bodies down manhole covers and into the sewer system. Those bodies floated out to the Detroit River and eventually into Lake Erie.

By the 1980s, city officials had pretty much given up trying to get Detroit back to its glory days of the 1950s. Coleman Young was in the middle of his 1974–1994 reign as Detroit mayor.

Young's first year in office saw 714 homicides in the city. That's still the record.

Everyone was on the take, especially the good guys. Detroit's longtime police chief was busted by the FBI with over six-hundred-thousand-dollar cash in a suspended ceiling in his basement.

Crack and gang crime riddled all corners of Detroit then. Instead of trying to root out the gangs, the city cut a deal with them. Detroit didn't have the political support or the law enforcement resources to fight the gangs anymore. The city's new attitude was "Don't kill civilians, and you can run all the drugs you want. Kill each other. We don't care. But if too many civilians get caught in the cross fire, we'll have to be involved." The gangs even left their own signature after a hit. The Mozambique pattern was a favorite of the Six-Mile Boys: two in the heart and one in the forehead. If you want to see a realistic look at what the drug trade in 1980s Detroit was like, check out the movie *White Boy Rick*. It's a true story.

There's a reason Dr. Jack Kevorkian established his personal brand as the Angel of Death in 1980s Detroit. Right to die by physician-assisted suicide was open for business.

With the Wild West playing out live across Detroit's 139 square miles, both Whites and Blacks continued to flee the city. At its financial zenith in the 1950s, Detroit City had a population of near two million people. By 1990, that had been cut in half to one million people (equal to the city's 1920 population). Now Detroit's population is well under seven hundred thousand and continuing to fall.

That flight meant more income and property tax dollars were leaving Detroit every year. The city couldn't pull out of the nosedive and finally crashed and burned in 2013. In roughly fifty years, Detroit had gone from the richest city in the United States to becoming the largest municipality in its history to declare bankruptcy.

I think about Southern Michigan University, which is a euphemism for the federal prison in Jackson, Michigan. Eastern, Western, Northern, and Central Michigan are all real universities spread out across the state. When you say someone is an alumnus of Southern, that means they spent time in Jackson's Federal Prison. As we used to say growing up, "I wouldn't fuck with that guy. He went to Southern."

Slade sees me starting out the window and asks, "You okay?" I hit him with the standard answer.

Sunday, November 17 at Michigan
Win 7–2

I'm *really okay* now. I get two goals from D, both on the power play! First one is on a beautiful face-off win by Chrisler. He drew it straight back to me, right on the tape, and I let it fly through a screen in front of Michigan goalie, Bill Perani. My family is there, of course, and they go crazy. It is always nice to win in the D.

It is a matinee game today. It starts at two. I stay over to have dinner with the family. We don't play again until Wednesday, so I'll fly back to Charlestowne the next morning on my own dime. My parents seem to get older every time I see them because I don't get to see them enough. Bad on me. I know I'll really regret that one day.

Monday, November 18

Sitting at the light on Rambler Road, waiting to make a left into the players' parking lot at Olympia Arena, I notice there is a new billboard ad right there at the intersection. You can see that billboard from either direction along Rambler Road. If you are stopped to make the left onto Olympia Arena property, it hits you right in the face. That billboard ad greets the boys every day when they arrive for practice or a game. And it greets the fans for every event at the arena.

This billboard ad has some of the highest nonfreeway traffic counts around Charlestowne. It dominates the street and parking lot entrance on that side of the building. The new billboard ad is from Bradberry's wife to him. It simply says, "Dear Pat Bradberry: Thanks for *everything*. Diana." Diana is the Baron of Brown's ex-wife. She cleaned him out in the divorce. Hardly any of us know how bad it was until today. She really twisted the knife with the billboard ad.

It's surprising to me that Pat got divorced. The Prince of Peach is so bland. I never thought he would rile up his wife enough where she would put him on irrevocable waivers. The Boss of Beige, fitting with his style, put it simply, "I was happily married for five years out of eleven. I guess that's not bad." The boys roar. Hogaboom starts to pass the hat for Bradberry. Some guys put in coins, some guys old hockey tape. Pittinger, Bradberry's partner forming the other half of our Brad Pitt defensive pairing, asks if it's too early to get Diana's cell number. Gallows humor.

Wednesday, November 20
Home versus North Jersey
Win 3–1

We have back-to-back wins again, second time in Yes-vember. Libbet's line has a strong game and accounts for all three goals. Hightower bags one with that patented oh-shit move on Gerry Coleman. Our defense shuts down the House Painters' potent offense. A great game for us at both ends of the ice. We need it to build some confidence. We really gotta get on a roll here.

Left wing Brody Cripenn plays a fantastic game for them. He does it all: kills penalties, blocks shots, and back-checks like a fiend. Cripenn also gets their only goal finishing off a beautiful give and go with Lyle Akouree. Both of them are pretty damn good hockey players.

Thursday, November 21

We have an enlightening geopolitical discussion after today's practice between Badinoff (Russia) and Budler (Czech Republic).

Budler says, "Hey, Boris! I hear your dad used to coach you as a kid. He coached hockey up there in that Siberia you are from for many years?"

Badinoff says, "Dah. Why you ask?"

Budler says, "My dad did the same: coached me and was a hockey coach a long time before that. Do you think our dads ever met?"

Badinoff says, "Yeah. Prague. Spring 1968."

That was the end of the Czechoslovakia Spring Uprising. The Russian Army invaded Prague, tightened down the Iron Curtain, and snapped it tight for another twenty-five years in fact.

Friday, November 22

Payday is every other Friday. Today, we're told if we can't wait until Monday to cash our checks (so the gate receipts from tomorrow's game will cover the payroll), then go see Tony over at the Backcheck Lounge. He'll cash it for you. *Vroom! Vroom!* Gentlemen, start your engines! It's the Indy 500 after practice. Guys race out of the arena parking lot to be one of the first to the Backcheck and get cashed out.

Before racing off to the Backcheck, a couple of people tell Lee Harvey, "Happy JFK Day." Very few of us under fifty years old get it. Sick? Well, I think the statute of comedy limitations expired on that one years go. It's been more than sixty years gone by since November 22, 1963. That day, however, was the end of an era. No more presidents riding around in open-top convertibles through a canyon of tall buildings!

I get to the Backcheck and get my payroll check cashed by Tony. I order some beers. The Backcheck is your classic dive bar. It's in a shitty part of town, pours cheap beer, and features morally flexible women. It also violates one of my cardinal rules when it comes to bars: *Don't go in if you can't see out.* Old Detroit street wisdom. There are no windows on the front side of the Backcheck. You can't see who is coming through the front door—makes me uncomfortable.

But the Backcheck is close to the arena and on the way home for most of the boys. And the cops know we hang out there, so they have our backs most of the time as long as you are not stupid.

Saturday, November 23
Home versus Michigan
Lose 5–2

I hate losing to Michigan, in Detroit, or here in Charlestowne. I get so frustrated, I challenge Command tough guy Tim Robertson at one point.

I say, "You wanna go? Or are those gloves glued on?"
Robertson says, "Scoreboard, fuck-tard."

Monday, November 25

We have a night off in Dallas before we play the Texas Marshalls Tuesday. I take some of the rookies (Badinoff, Steele, and Crosby) to dinner at Bob's Steak and Chop House (the original on Lemmon Avenue downtown, not the poser places in the suburbs). Then we hit a Pink Floyd tribute concert by the cover band Pink Cecil. That's the rookie's price for a free steak dinner.

They have no idea who Pink Floyd is. I tell them that *The Dark Side of the Moon* is not only one of the most critically acclaimed albums in the history of music. It is also one of the greatest-selling albums of all time. "What the fuck is an album?" is their response.

I try and explain *The Dark Side of the Moon* was on the Billboard Top 100 LPs and tape list for 950 weeks. That's over eighteen years! *The Dark Side of the Moon* sold over forty-five million albums, putting them number 4 all time in album sales. In the history of music, only Michael Jackson, AC/DC, and Meat Loaf had single albums that sold more copies than *The Dark Side of the Moon*.

Oh, Michael Jackson! They nod knowingly at that name.

I give up. I decide not to talk about Pink Floyd's *Animals* album. The song "Pigs (Three Different Ones)" was my jam before I would hit the ice in juniors. A man next to us at the concert is wearing a T-shirt featuring the album cover from *Wish You Were Here*. I point to the guy *not* on fire and tell the rookies, "That is me. I posed for that picture." The rookies fall for it. Dopes. The guy *not* on fire looks a lot like I did back in the day. I still get a lot of mileage out of telling people I'm the guy on the cover of *Wish You Were Here* who is *not* on fire. But no one ever does the math. The album came out almost fifty years ago.

Tuesday, November 26 at Texas
Lose 4–3

Our game is secondary news in Icemen land. There was an assassination today in Dallas.

The owner's kid, Barron Richard Ruthlessberger (B R-squared) is on this team trip. He's a big-time jock sniffer. Our players buddy up to him and use B R-squared as a way to get messages to his dad, going around the coaches. That drives Barnes crazy. That's why I knew I had to warn Barnes that the boy was on this trip with guests.

The guests of B R-squared are two guys from DePasto Oldsmobile (the Icemen auto dealership sponsor), two from the Charlestowne Budweiser distributor, and two guests from City Hall. All seven went wild hog hunting this morning before our game against Texas. It sounds kinda cool. You take a helicopter about fifty miles southwest of Dallas. There is some private land out there where you can hunt wild hogs from the chopper using side-mounted .50 calibers. Halfway through the hunt, as they are closing in on a two hundred pounder, the chopper makes a slight bank left.

One of the City Hall guests falls out. Meanwhile, the other City Hall guest is firing away at the hog with the .50 caliber. Not only does the fall fuck up City Hall guest number 1, he gets hit by .50 caliber shrapnel courtesy of City Hall guest number 2. He dies on the way to the hospital back in Dallas.

The dead City Hall guest turns out to be a Charlestowne city council member who voted against construction of the new arena. The guy who accidently shot him is a political lobbyist who ran point on financing the biggest part of the new arena construction: working with the Chinese Government on the notoriously shady EB-5 visa/ immigration financing.

He shot him accidently as in I-accidently-stabbed-the-guy-seven-times type of accident. More likely, the city council member had some dirt on the whys and hows the new arena was getting built.

And who was taking the cash kickbacks from the mob and the Chinese? Dead men tell no tales.

The boys has a field day with this, typical hockey locker room humor. Slade asks Lee Harvey where he was this afternoon, like a he's a suspect. Lee Harvey says, "I beat the bishop [jacked off] and then took a nap. Check my hotel room for DNA, Mr. NCIS Charlestowne!"

Seriously, though, a political opponent of the new arena accidently falls out of a helicopter while hunting wild hogs. And then is accidently killed by friendly fire from one of the other hunters who just happens to have run the financing operation. This is right out of the Vito Corleone playbook. We're only missing a severed horse head under the bedsheets and Clemenza unloading a couple of shotgun blasts into a full elevator. Leave the gun. Take the cannoli!

Wednesday, November 27

A day before Thanksgiving, the hotel is pretty empty except for out-of-towners visiting family in the Dallas area for Thanksgiving. At a hotel bar that night, Hogaboom entertains us with a twenty-dollar bill attached to some six-pound test fishing line. He throws the twenty dollars out onto the walkway outside the bar. As soon as someone bends over to pick it up, Boomer yanks on the clear fishing line and snatches the bill back. Then the boys yell, "Fuck! Boomer! For fuck's sake!"

It was funny the first seventeen times Boomer did it. Damn, I am easily amused.

Thursday, November 28

We have the team Thanksgiving meal in a Tech City hotel ballroom. The game tomorrow is against the Lazers.

I get to talk in depth with Jeffrey Karvaala for first time this season about something besides hockey. The Finlander has solid fundamentals but really shines on defense. His dad, Toivo, coached him as a kid growing up and it shows. Toivo was the head of the Fin's national program for years. Jeff learned well from Dad. Jeff is a speedy back-checker who always has his man in the defensive zone. For us, he plays right wing on the Craigsen line. Jeff's not afraid to use the stick on someone either—typical gritty Fin work ethic. Dad is very proud of him.

Karvaala doesn't understand the concept of American Thanksgiving. First, the fact US retail starts to stock Thanksgiving items *before* Halloween now plus all the food and the football. It boggles his mind when I tell him with all the Canadians sitting close by listening intently that Canada has their own Thanksgiving in October. His mind is blown. Me too. I have to admit. Columbus didn't discover Nova Scotia, did he? I thought Columbus landed at

Plymouth Rock. Or was that the Mayflower and the Pilgrims? Fuck it. Pass the sweet potatoes, please.

Jeff and I do talk about Christmas and how it gets tough for a guy like him to be away from family. There is a union mandated break for the players around Christmas but nowhere enough time to get to Finland and back.

Karvaala tells me Christmas goes by the name Hyvää joulua in Finland and that is their big-meal event. Lutefish (salt fish) is the traditional starter. The main meal is a leg of pork served with mashed potato traditionally baked slowly in birchbark boxes in the oven. Casseroles containing different vegetables including, rutabaga, carrot, and potato are also common.

Karvaala gets Christmas. He's a big fan. He tells me that Santa Claus lives in the north part of Finland called Korvatunturi (or Lapland), north of the Arctic Circle. People from all over the world send letters to Santa Claus in Finland. There is a big tourist theme park called Christmas Land in the north of Finland near to where they say that Santa lives and Karvaala grew up.

That means Santa doesn't have far to travel on Christmas Eve to deliver presents to people in Finland! Whoop! Whoop!

It gets dark very early, about 3:00 p.m., in most parts of Finland at Christmas. It's now traditional to go to cemeteries and visit the graves of family members. Some cemeteries are enormous, and police are on duty to manage the traffic, but everyone must walk the last few yards to the grave. Candles in hanging lanterns are left around the grave. The whole cemetery is alight with glowing lanterns shining in the snow—a winter wonderland Karvaala says. He sighs. Jeff is drifting back to the homeland in his mind, thinking about Toivo and his mother, Vienna. He smiles. So do I.

Friday, November 29 at Tech City
Lose 4–2

Tonight's loss gives us a 4-7-1 record for *No*-vember. We only managed two wins after November 6. Something has to give or we'll be out of it by Christmas. We are eighteen points out of fourth place in the eight-team East division. That's still a solid last place.

Only the top four teams in the division make the playoffs. We have a 7-15-2 record after first twenty-four games or roughly one-third of the season gone. That's only sixteen out of a possible forty-eight points. Holy shit! That's a debacle.

CHAPTER 4

Bench Clearers, Holiday Cheer,
and the Iron Lung

Sunday, December 1 at Cleveland
Win 6–2

Before our game, DeMarko is bragging about an earlier trip to Cleveland. This piece of shit took a Steamers front office *intern* to a Cavs game, got her drunk, and then pounded her for forty-five minutes on a couch in the Steamers offices. He's reliving the NBA crowd noise coming through the office walls. "They were applauding and that kept me going. Couple of times, I could feel the crowd anticipating something big. They would go, 'Ah. Ah.' I would get a toehold, drive as deep as I could, and make her cum when the crowd exploded in celebration."

He shares one of his favorite sayings to the group listening, "It's like I always say, boys. Don't sweat the petty things. Just pet the sweaty things." Wow. I bet your wife and kids are proud of you. One thing I am a big believer in about this life: What goes around comes around. DeMarko will get his comeuppance one day.

Wednesday, December 4
Home versus Peninsula
Win 4–2

We make great effort in front of the home fans. Of all people, Steele gets the empty netter to seal it. His Twitter blows up postgame. Hogaboom sets up the third goal, the GWG by Libbet, with a huge open ice check in the neutral zone. He catches Panthers' speedy winger, Geoff Murcer, with his head down, looking back over his shoulder for a pass. As soon as Murcer gets the puck and starts to look up ice, he gets kaboomed. Hogey hits him fair, square, and hard. Murcer's equipment goes flying everywhere. Both gloves, his helmet, and his stick are scattered over the left side of center ice. On the bench, Hawkes yells excitingly, "Boomtown yard-saled that guy! Hey, Murcer! Get your shit back at the yard sale in boomtown."

This game has it all for a Wednesday night. Section 8 gets the crowd going early and gets into Peninsula's heads too. Panthers' Albert MacKartnee dresses as the backup goalie for them. On the bench, he is within a couple of feet of the Section 8 crazies all night. MacKartnee is down on the farm from his NHL team for a couple of games, fresh out of a thirty-day rehab stay for Coke. The first three rows of Section 8 all bring to the game clear plastic bags with a white powder in it and wave those bags at MacKartnee all game long. The Panthers' players are pissed.

The main event featuring Hawkes comes early—about halfway into the first period. You could tell by the chatter in warm-up that Hawkes is going to stalk Peninsula's Bob Slydell until he catches him. Slydell trash-talked Hawkes about three weeks ago when we played in Peninsula. He called One Punch all kinds of derogatory names related to his Inuit heritage. Now comes time for Slydell to walk the walk, not just talk the talk.

His walk is short-lived. Slydell is in his own zone, far right corner battling with Budler for the puck. Hawkes sees his opening. He leaves his spot about halfway up the boards on the right side and goes charging elbows high into Slydell. It should have been a penalty, but the refs aren't stupid (well, most of them aren't stupid). They know

80

the history between these guys. It got picked up by a lot of hockey bloggers. The refs know Hawkes and Slydell are going to go sometime in this game. The refs figure, "Let's get it over early."

Slydell gets up off his ass, his whole backside full of snow he picked up sliding into the corner. Nothing is said. The gloves come off, and both players tug up on their elbow pads to make sure nothing gets in the way of punching.

In the last three weeks, Slydell obviously did his due diligence on Hawkes. He knew to avoid that right hand like the buffet at a leper's convention. The linesmen keep their distance. They get it too. There will be no intervention until someone hits the ice. Slydell rains five or six rights down on Hawkes looking for the early KO. Hawkes takes those shots without flinching. Slydell is getting tired. Hawkes shakes his right arm free of Slydell's clenched left hand. Hawkes fires a decent right on the button, and now he has Slydell worried. You can see it in his eyes. Hawkes cocks his right back *way* past his right ear, like a baseball catcher getting ready to throw out a baserunner at second. Slydell's eyes get big. He's seeing the flash of a nuclear bomb right before the heat, and the wave vaporizes you two seconds later. Hawkes hits Slydell with a monstrous straight right, first makes contact where the front edge of Slydell's helmet meets his forehead. Slydell's helmet pops off his head and goes ten feet straight up in the air. With the follow-through, Hawkes slides down from the initial helmet popper and crushes the bridge of Slydell's nose. It's like a faucet is turned wide open. Suddenly, Slydell has a dent in his forehead and a nose so flat he could bite a wall. Postgame surgery is on his late-night menu.

Friday, December 6
Home versus Old Market
Lose 1–0

I don't understand our team. We should have parlayed all that energy from the Peninsula win to beat this mediocre Old Market team, especially in our own barn. We are so inconsistent. Fucking schizophrenic. It should be the Charlestowne Sybils.

We get shut out *at home* by Lancers' goalie, Elmer Hackareinin. Early on, it looked like one of those games where one goal might hold up. It did. We get nothing past this guy. How old is fucking Hackareinin? Elmer is so old, he still owes Fred Flintstone fifty bucks. Retire, you old fuck.

Sunday, December 8
Home versus Gotham
Lose 5–4 in overtime

Another frustrating loss. We get a point for getting to OT but still, we need some Ws badly.

The line of the night from Metros center, Stephan Ryan, to Budler as they are lining up across from each other for a face-off: "That's a nice helmet. Does it come in man's size too?" Budler does wear one of those funky Eastern European brain buckets from Jofa. A vintage-looking helmet that Gretzky made famous. Ryan apparently doesn't know he's beaking a stone-cold killer. It's a close game, so Budler ignores Ryan. Lucky Ryan.

Tuesday, December 10

Bus to North Jersey. DeMarko is sitting in his normal spot, row two left side, right behind me. He's doing some game prep already for tomorrow night. DeMarko starts going through his fight slang: starched, snot locker, Chiclets, fed him a left for lunch, turtled, etc. He must be the perverted reincarnation of Nostradamus. Tomorrow night, he would need *all* the hockey fight terms he could think of and then some.

Wednesday, December 11 at North Jersey
Lose 5–2

It's a tight back-and-forth game. We're down 2–1, then tie it 2–2 on a shorthanded goal by Slade. We fall behind 3–2 midway through the second. Early in the third period, two awful penalty calls go against us—total home cooking by the officials. We give up back-to-back power play goals, and suddenly, we're trailing North Jersey 5–2 with six minutes left in the game. We're done.

The proverbial shit hits the fan soon after the House Painters' fifth goal. With the game pretty much settled, their goon of a defenseman, Aedan Becker, nails Hightower in the face with a vicious elbow. Becker is an Irish-German mouth-breathing, ginger-haired fucker with one brown and one blue eye. In other words, a freak. He nails Lee Harvey so hard, even the North Jersey home crowd collectively goes, "Oh." There is no penalty called! WTF! Are you kidding me? These refs are consistent, consistently bullshit.

Hightower is stunned, hurt. He's lying on his left side and holding his head. Slade jumps Becker, and they start to trade hands. The other players on the ice square off. Even goalies Crosby and Bob Ennet (not to be confused with brother Bill Ennet) have discarded masks, gloves, and blockers, each holding a significant piece of the other's jersey. After a couple of minutes, even they start to throw. Crosby is holding his own in what I'm sure is his first hockey fight *ever*! But then the extra North Jersey player, who is unoccupied because Hightower is hurt, comes over and starts punching a defenseless Crosby in the face while Ennet keeps his arms pinned. We won't stand for that—can't.

Hammer jumps off our bench to even things out, followed quickly by Bradberry and Hogaboom. North Jersey sees what's happening so they stream off their bench. Quicker than you can say, "Bench-clearing brawl," every Icemen and House Painter player is on the ice and engaged in a good old-fashioned Pier 6 street fight.

This goes on for ten minutes maybe, the refs, linesmen, and eventually some North Jersey Police trying to separate the players on the ice. All the fans' eyes are focused there. Suddenly, there's a commotion behind our bench.

I turn to look. I'm stunned. A whole section of glass behind our bench is missing—the glass that separates the first row of fans from the players on the bench. Our trainer, Chuck Hartnett, is up in the first row of the stands fighting a couple of North Jersey fans! I am tied up with one of the Barbour twins on the ice. (Billy? Bobby?

Thelma? Louise? Fucking twins.) I shake him loose and speed toward our bench to help Chuck. Other Icemen have the same idea. Before I get there, Budler, Steele, and Hammer are already in the stands with Chuck. Hammer is pummeling some fat fifty-year-old in a Becker House Painters jersey. When I arrive, we have seven to eight players plus Chuck up in the first two rows of the stands, going hand to hand with North Jersey fans. Barnes is standing behind our group and pointing at fans screaming, "That one! Get that fucker!" At some point, I notice the fighting on the ice has stopped. The eighteen North Jersey players and our eight players *not* in the stands are just holding onto each other and watching in complete amazement. So are the game officials. The NJPD, who were on the ice trying to restore order when the benches cleared, are now attempting to get between angry fans and Icemen. Traffic-control cops from the parking lots, wearing their bright-orange vests, have approached the melee from the stands. They are trying to flank the group fighting at our bench. Traffic-control cops are swinging those heavy industrial flashlights that they all carry. Out of the corner of his eye, Hammer sees someone wearing orange closing on him quickly and carrying a long object. In a riot like this (especially in the other guys' arena), you keep your head on a swivel. Shoot first. Ask questions later. Hammer has no time to ascertain the threat level coming in from his right. He takes his hockey stick and with a big two-handed thrust forward, spears the oncoming person right in the groin. That person falls immediately and disappears behind the seats in row three.

It takes police and arena security at least a half hour to separate everyone and restore some semblance of order. Once that happens, the referees immediately send both teams to their respective locker rooms so they can straighten out the penalty calls. That takes another thirty minutes. When the refs finally have the official penalty calls ready to announce, they realize something: There is less than six minutes left to play in a 5–2 game. With the number of penalty minutes from the fight, including numerous ten-minute game and gross misconducts, both teams have barely enough players left to play six on six. Let alone put together enough bodies to play out the final six minutes. Then there is the risk of restarting the game, more fights, and the fans' emotions flaring up.

Referees call the game after talking to the AHA Commissioner, Steve Archer. North Jersey wins 5–2.

With the game called early, we undress, shower, pack up gear, and tend to our wounds. There is a knock on the locker room door. Strange. Most people who need to be in the locker room just walk right in. No one knocks. Is it North Jersey players? Is it North Jersey hockey front-office types looking to smoke the peace pipe? Who knows? But everyone looks at me 'cause I'm standing next to the door.

I open it after a third knock. It's a dozen or so of North Jersey's finest: po-po, policia, five-o, bacon, barneys, law enforcement, and the man.

I innocently say, "Gentlemen! Well, that was a real gong show of a hockey game, huh? What can we do for you?"

The police captain, glowering, says, "Where's twenty-eight? He's going nowhere. He's staying with us."

I, feigning shock, say, "Twenty-eight. Lufthammer. I'm his coach. Why do you want to see him?"

The police captain says, "Where should I start? Simple assault. Assault with a deadly weapon. Assaulting a police officer. Need more? 'Cause there will be more."

I say, "Holy shit! I think he's in the shower. Let me check."

The police captain says, "You've got two minutes. After that, we are coming in to get him."

I close the door. The whole locker room sees what had just transpired. Hammer is halfway dressed and back by the showers combing his hair. The boys purposely keep him out of sight. There's only one escape from this one. I trot over to Hammer. He knows he's fucked and going to jail. Or maybe not. I've got an idea. "Okay, big boy," I say to him. "Into the stick bag you go." At first, he doesn't get it. Then he twigs in. He smiles from ear to ear. So does Sal, our equipment guy. Their faces look like they have just been given the winning lottery numbers two days out. The boys load Hammer into the biggest stick bag. Similar to a military body bag, it's plenty long for a body and zips right up—no plastic windows to see what's in the bag. There is another knock at the door. Is two minutes up already? I go to the door.

I say, "I've looked all over, even on the bus. Number 28 must have slipped out into the night already."

The captain says, "Don't mind if we look around?" He elbows his way past me.

"Please," I say while making a sweeping gesture.

I want to say, "Let's see your warrant," but I don't. NJPD is not in a mood to be fucked with. NJPD looks in the showers, in the shitters, medical room, visiting coaches' office, and various closets. Meanwhile Icemen players keep dressing and heading to the bus. Sal and Chuck move the equipment out to the bus including one very special stick bag. Bus is now loaded and ready to go. NJPD stops us as we leave the loading dock. They board the bus still looking for Hammer. They check every seat and the bathroom. They check briefly under the bus in the storage hold where the Icemen's equipment sits. They flashlight the space but don't open any bags. Twenty miles down the road, our bus pulls over. We open the storage hold and let Hammer out of the stick bag. His first words were "I fought the law, and I WON! Somebody fucking beer me. By the way, this stick bag fucking STINKS."

Thursday, December 12

Our bench clearer in North Jersey is the talk of the hockey world. Unfortunately, the biggest voice in that conversation is AHA Commissioner Archer. Barnes, Icemen GM Lakor, and I have to hustle to Old Market first thing this morning to meet the commish at an Old Town Hotel.

By 1:00 p.m., we're walking to the hotel boardroom to watch a video of the bench clearer. The video is supplied by North Jersey. It's shot by the guy who does their coaches' video. Coaches' videos are a teaching tool, not framed and shot tight for TV highlights. They are framed and shot wide so the coach can see the whole ice as can the Commissioner, unfortunately for us.

I'm working Commish Archer as we get ready to watch the video, lobbying the best I can to downplay the night before.

I say, "You know North Jersey, Steve. They always exaggerate. They hate us. The fight wasn't as bad as they're telling you. They are trying to fuck us with fines and suspensions. I wouldn't be surprised if they didn't ask for the death penalty for Hammer!"

The commish says, "Have you seen the video?"

I say, "Err. No."

The commish says, "Then I wouldn't say another fucking word until you see the video."

The commish drops an f-bomb on me. This is not good.

The video begins. It shows the start of the fights on the ice and the benches clearing. Ten minutes into the video, the camera pans away from the ice and zooms in on the Icemen bench area. We see Chuck wrestling with the glass behind the bench, removing it from the stanchions and throwing the glass up into the crowd. (We don't see what set Chuck off. Like the Zapruder film, the guy shooting the coaches' video for the House Painters gets part of his shot obstructed. Kennedy was behind the freeway-entrance sign when the first bullet hit him. But when JFK emerged from behind that sign, he had both hands up around his own throat, like he was choking himself. He'd been hit by the first shot. And like Zapruder, the guy shooting the coaches' video also missed getting on tape the first shot of Chuck versus the fans.)

All the gory details now spill out on the hotel big screen TV. Chuck, by himself, was fighting fans in row one. Budler, Steele, Slade, and Hammer were soon climbing from the bench to the stands to help Chuck followed by me. And then comes the kill shot. Barnes is standing on our bench behind the Icemen players in the seats, pointing and yelling at a fan. When none of the Icemen react to Barnes's pleas to go after the fan he's pointing to, Barnes decides if you want a job done right, do it yourself. He runs to the other end of our bench, grabs a stick out of the stick rack, and races back to the fight. Barnes climbs into row one. Leaping above Slade and Budler, he uses the hockey stick as a big fly swatter. He strikes the fan twice on the head and shoulders. Seconds after Barnes' second blow on that fan, we clearly see Hammer draw back his stick and spear a North Jersey police officer in the nuts.

Watching this train wreck of a video unfold in slow motion, I catch Commish Archer glancing back at me with a look of pure disdain. I can read his mind, "See, asshole? Don't run your spin game on me ever again unless you've watched the video."

Barnes, Lakor, and I know we're fucked. Suspensions and fines will be coming. We head back to Old Market and check into the hotel. The boys are in hotel bar waiting to greet us. Every one of them is wearing those novelty fake glasses with the big nose and moustache. They look like they're in the witness protection program or posing as a Hanson brother. Good thing they still have a sense of humor. I remind them, "PLEASE no social media comments on the brawl with North Jersey. We are facing fines, suspensions, and maybe even arrest warrants."

They can't wait to tell Barnes and me about practice that morning. There are no coaches at our practice because Barnes and I are headed to a meeting with the commish. Captain Libbet runs practice. After practice with no adults in the locker room, the boys commandeer a briefcase Steele always has with him. Triple-6 thinks the briefcase gives him an air of intelligence and business savvy. Four guys hold Steele back while Hogaboom and a couple of other veterans gleefully open the briefcase to see what industrial and state secrets it holds. The briefcase content consists solely of one Milky Way candy bar, a *Daily Racing Form*, and a three-year-old Penthouse. Not a pad of paper or pen anywhere. The boys laugh their asses off. I'm wary as they tell me the story. That's a dangerous maneuver considering Steele is as crazy as a shithouse raccoon and three times as dangerous.

Friday, December 13 at Old Market
Lose 4–1

With the craziest fans in the AHA (yes, even worse than our own Section 8), Old Market is a tough place to play at any time— let alone on Friday the thirteenth. All the chaos and bedlam coming from their fans fires up the Lancers. On our bench, the tank is empty—all emotion spent after the fight with North Jersey. Mr. Hockey addresses us before the game about sticking together as a team, both fighting and playing hockey together. He drops a new term on us: Ferda. As in do it fer da boys. We love it, but it doesn't help. We literally go down without a fight, 4–1.

Sunday, December 15

The boys are still buzzing about the Jersey joust from four days ago. The suspended guys are still practicing. I finally find out what started the melee. A North Jersey fan reached over the glass and pulled Chuck's hair. Chuck snapped, pulled the glass loose from the stanchion, and went up into the stands to get the guy. Subsequent events including our Icemen players in the stands fighting Jersey fans were forever captured in glorious VHS color.

Monday, December 16
Home versus Great Lakes
Win 4–1

Barnes is serving the first of his two-game suspension for the New Jersey brawl. I'm head coach for tonight and Thursday's game at Peninsula.

This being the first home game after the bench clearer, Hammer chants from the crowd are big. The stick-bag story is out there. Some fan from Section 8 comes dressed as a stick bag, a hole conveniently cut so he can watch tonight's game. Hammer chants go on all game, but he's not even dressed. He is suspended for three games: tonight, at Peninsula Thursday, and then the January 28 game back in North Jersey. I'm okay with the January 28 ban. There will probably be a warrant waiting for him anyway.

Hawkes fights their tough guy, Patsy Lowry. You can see them talking to each other during the shift. At the next face-off comes this exchange.

Hawkes says, "You wanna go, Irish?"

Lowry says, "You're damn right I do."

Hawkes says with real sincerity, "Well, then. Good luck to ya."

No KO, but Hawkes wins a unanimous decision. He also gets a goal and an assist—the Gordie Howe hat trick for Hawkes!

Tuesday, December 17

"FUCK! BOOMER! FOR FUCK'S SAKES!" Hogaboom pranks the rookies this time. He puts a piece of clear scotch tape across their skate blades. Only in a couple of spots but that's enough. Walking on the rubber mats from our locker room to the ice, you don't notice. As soon as you hit the ice, though, and part of your blade is not touching ice because of tape, down you go.

While pretending to be on his cell, Hogey videos the whole thing and uploads it to his Twitter. Within minutes, the tweet has several hundred views.

Wednesday, December 18

Kids, wake up Mom and Dad! It's time for our monthly educational interlude we like to call *Icemen hockey insider lesson of the month*. This month's lesson: navigating the booster club class system.

Before we get rolling, allow me to pontificate. What is a booster club? What is their primary function? The booster club is made up of your diest of die-hard fans. They literally have Icemen tattoos and attend every home game and many road games. If they can't make a booster club bus trip to a road game, they'll certainly listen to every minute of DeMarkos radio broadcast.

All are season ticket holders (that's a prerequisite to join). Many are Section 8ers. Almost all are small business owners or employees of a small business. They are the backbone of so many things in Charlestowne and across the USA.

The booster club carries forward to the public the importance of the Icemen in our community: financially, emotionally, and spiritually. The Icemen are part of the social fabric of Charlestowne. That is the creed the booster club goes by.

They are also our go-to group for free labor. The Icemen business side is not very big, maybe fifteen full-timers. The game night labor needs are filled by interns and the booster club. The boosters are perfect to handle a giveaway to the fans, either on ingress or egress. That way, they can be in their seats and see almost all the game. It's harder to get their help during the game, like intermissions. Booster club bodies are invaluable for executing promotions in and around Charlestowne: autograph appearances, charity work, school, and classroom youth programs, etc.

Like most organizations, the booster club has a distinct pecking order.

Tier one. Booster club board of directors (aka the elites).

The board is usually five to six people: a president, a couple of VPs, treasurer, event person (helps at paid or sponsor events), and a charity person (helps at nonpaying philanthropic events). They are senior to the other booster club members in terms of age, tenure, status, and political infighting skills.

The current president is Lynda Robinson. A former puck bunny is now too old to get the players' attention but still hot enough to sleep with both the owner's son (B R-Squared) and Mayor Vizzyello.

Tier two. Fans are in it just for the hockey (aka puck nerds).

Two distinct subgroups here. Old media nerds. Older fans that get to Olympia Arena before warm-up starts, so they can chart the lines. They buy a game program and keep score *every* game. The have kept every game program of their lives. They don't follow hockey closely outside Charlestowne and the AHA. These older puck nerds will be among the most emotional when this final Icemen season ends. Many have family memberships to the booster club to include their kids. Some were kids twenty to thirty years ago when Dad first signed them up.

New media nerds (younger, under thirty years old for sure). They're fantasy hockey, esports, and video-game types. Their hockey knowledge comes mostly from playing Sega, Nintendo, and EA Sports NHL games on PlayStation and Xbox. They certainly know more about NHL player's stats from video games than they do from going to real games or watching on TV.

The younger puck nerds have little social life but do like to drink beer. So many of them join the boosters and go to the games as a group. They are *not* Section 8 material.

Tier three. These are female groupies looking to hook up with players (aka puck bunnies).

Dressed to kill in the Arena Club after every home game. They run in packs like she wolves. Puck bunnies have two main nesting areas: Arena Club postgame and at the Backcheck Lounge all other times, including post practice. They include proud participants in Hog Thursday. These are the fans that hope that standing next to a player at the car dealership while he is signing autographs will lead to her being rear-ended afterward. Player tunnel buddies run rampant with this demo.

Tier four: These are male fans looking to hook up with puck bunnies (aka sloppy seconders).

Much like the jungle hyenas that clean up the scraps after the lions have feasted, this group has no illusions about their status level. They don't bother to hit on the puck bunnies right away. They wait until almost all players have left the bar or made their selection. Then the sloppy seconders move in to try and pick up the heartbroken and the extremely drunk.

This male demo sadly runs eighteen to fifty years old. There is some advantage to being old and rich but not as fat as Jabba the Hutt. This tier includes some of the Icemen front office staff, especially ticket sales kids. They take sloppy seconds and brag about it.

Coming up. January's *Icemen hockey insider lesson of the month*: the hockey sex glossary.

Thursday, December 19 at Peninsula
Lose 7–1

No Barnes or Lufthammer again. Steele and Budler are suspended too. We play two men short because of the suspensions. I actually coach *and* dress—play a shift here and there to give the boys a break. Our owners are too cheap to sign a couple of free agents to a PTO (pro tryout) to fill in until the suspensions are over. Pittinger pulls a flamingo early in the game. Instead of blocking a Lou Penzeen shot with his skate, Pitt Flamingoed. He lifts his foot as the shot went by. Crosby has been screened until then. He never has a chance to visually pick up the shot. We didn't have a chance either. We get our asses kicked 7–1. We get outcoached. Nah. Just sucked.

Our worst game of the year. Guys looked like they were already on their four-day Christmas break. I have to admit I'm looking forward to it.

Friday, December 20

Barnes and I get called into GM Lakor's office after practice. Our female masseuse has told ownership she plans to sue the team and Craigsen for sexual harassment. She claims Craigsen farts on her every time she touches his legs right on cue every time. The other players and staff in the trainer's room think it's hilarious.

(Hockey players and poo humor. It might make a good Icemen hockey insider lesson of the month.) The masseuse of course is appalled and humiliated.

Lakor asks us to talk to Craigsen. "Tell him to stop farting on the masseuse." Sure, we'll talk to Cake Boss about his rectal turbulence. I say, "No problem."

This is what I wanted to say but didn't: "What the fuck? He's your boy, Lakor. I knew this guy was going to be a cancer. Doesn't want to be in Charlestowne. Doesn't want to work hard. Doesn't care about his teammates. And now getting the organization sued. What a fucking loser. And we are stuck with him. No way Springfield will take him back. Nice acquisition, GM of the year."

Saturday, December 21
Home versus Tech City
Win 6–2

Barnes is back behind the bench and not soon enough. I still have to dress and play forward, but we will be pretty much suspension free after tonight. Just the Hammer game next month in North Jersey is left on the court docket.

We chase Lazers all-star goalie, Brad Schultz, early. He is off on his angles, and Hightower catches him twice showing too much net. Badinoff and Slade get one each on Schultz before they mercifully pull him.

The fans cheer hard for that sixth goal. Karvaala gets the sixth, and everyone goes home with visions of free french fries from Bumpa's Burgers dancing in their heads.

Monday, December 23 at Elmdale
Win 3–2

We get some unexpected offense from Steele tonight, a goal and an assist! Zeleski is not really tested but does what he has to do. We've suddenly won three out of our last four games and picked up six points in the division standings. We are going into the four-day Christmas break on a very high note.

December 24–27

Christmas break.

Wednesday, December 25

I have the six players with nowhere to go over for Christmas dinner. I don't cook. Three of the booster club ladies cook it up for me in the morning and deliver to my house all wrapped in tin. It's quite the eclectic mix of Icemen that sit down to turkey and mashed potatoes: Badinoff, Hogaboom, Karvaala, Budler, Hawkes, and Steele. It's the fucking United Nations! Karvaala is especially grateful. He loves everything about Christmas. The boys entertain themselves with Call of Duty, Grand Theft Auto, and Fortnite on my PS6. I let them game. They are back in their parents' basements at this moment.

I chip in with stories from AHA past. They love the one about the linesman, still wearing his skates, chasing a fan through the stands, down the concourse, and out into the parking lot. A fan has thrown an empty liquor bottle at the referee and knocks him out cold on the ice. Christ, that must be thirty years ago at least. It happened in Old Town, of course—that shithole.

Steele shares a story from his college frat house days. Triple-6 and his Phi Sig brothers play a game they called chemical roulette. Phi Sigs would remove the labels from their prescription drug bottles, mix up all the pills, distribute handfuls to themselves and party guests, and wash it down with a concoction the Greeks called sea breeze. There is no specific recipe outside white liquor only (gin or vodka), soda, fruit juices, and fruit slices. They would literally mix up dozens of bottles into a fifty-gallon trash can and serve. Most drink out of a red solo cup. Some of the crazies like Steele would dip an empty fifth bottle into the trash can, fill 'er up, and wander around the party in some drug-alcohol stupor that would have embarrassed Hunter S. Thompson. Steele is seriously warped. I wonder if we can get through the season with him before something *really bad* happens.

Thursday, December 26

Section 8 has their Christmas party at the Backcheck Lounge. I make a brief appearance but leave before things get too wound up. Section 8 fans have a Marine mentality versus regular fans who have an Army attitude. Section 8 lives by kill them all, let God sort them out, or as Slade would echo: take no prisoners and shoot the wounded.

Bottom line is that Section 8 fans have more passion than anyone else. That helps explain (to a certain extent) the November incident where Section 8 fans crossed over to the other side of the arena, got down behind our bench, and pounded on the glass while screaming at the Icemen. They are a positive influence all season long on the players, the city, and on other fans. Their fire has fueled Icemen playoff runs in the past. There are long-term generational ties between Section 8 and past teams. Section 8's journey this final season will be nostalgic and sad—memory provoking for fathers, sons, moms, and daughters.

The Kenyan brothers are here, of course. They sit first row above the visiting players' tunnel.

Craigsen is here too. I find out later Craigsen arrived right as I was leaving. He had gotten back from Ontario that afternoon. It is an unexpected move by Craigsen to attend this party. Maybe his family had a coming-to-Jesus discussion with him over Christmas and urged him to make the best of his time in Charlestowne.

At the party, Craigsen strikes up a conversation with an older man, Dr. Frederic Modato. Doc is our unofficial mental health coach. He's paid by our NHL club to periodically wander the Icemen offices and locker room and ask deep-penetrating questions like "How ya doing, kid?" I love Dr. Modato. He has a wicked dark sense of humor.

Years ago, he asked me after a particularly hard loss, "How ya doing, kid?"

"Not good," I replied.

"I'm depressed and don't feel like myself."

Dr. Modato says, "Just remember, Vito. You're never alone with a schizophrenic."

Classic line, even if stolen from Ian Hunter.

According to our mascot (Cappeletti), Craigsen spends a good hour talking to Modato. Cappeletti talks to Craigsen right afterward, and Mr. Sulking seems inspired by the doc. I hope so. That would be a Christmas (and coaches') miracle come true.

Friday, December 27

All the players are back in town tonight, the last night of the Christmas break. A tradition since he's been an Icemen player, his Icemen teammates all gather at Tony Richatelli's family bar for a private holiday party.

The Richatelli family takes great pride in hosting this Christmas get-together every year almost as much pride as they have in son, Tony. Born and raised in Charlestowne, former Icemen stick boy who played his amateur hockey right here in C-Towne, Tony is now a regular pro with the Icemen. Tony Sr. and family pay for the whole evening: food, alcohol, and entertainment. They have a live band, Geneva. Geneva is a great rock-and-roll party band. Working the room is traveling entertainment like magicians and card-trick experts. The Icemen players bring wives and/or girlfriends if they want. (But not both.)

Badinoff isn't old enough to legally drink in the US. He's only nineteen. But they grow up quickly in the Oblast region of Russia. He's been drinking vodka for seven years already. Tonight, he drinks too much vodka. It was obvious all night long that Boris was having a good time, being overserved as we like to say. But, hey, it's the players' blowout before the second half sprint starts.

No one is driving. The players all have taxi chits to get home and even some of the booster club is on hand to provide rides if needed. We all knew Boris is getting more hammered than Bob Vila's left thumb. But we think he'd be a good Russian, go home, and sleep it off.

The party is winding down around 1:00 a.m. A clearly intoxicated Badinoff is talking to Amy Richatelli, Tony's twenty-year-old sister. Off the corner of the bar, Badinoff tries to kiss her and gets the Heisman from Amy. Now he goes all in. Boris pulls up her sweater and starts to stroke her breasts and kiss her stomach. Amy pushes him away. She's knows it's the Ketel One talking.

But Badinoff won't stop. Now he puts his right hand down her pants, and *bam*, we've just crossed into sexual-assault territory. Amy screams and still can't get loose from the 6'2" and 210-pound teen. Richatelli now sees what is going on and comes to his sister's rescue. Tony bounds across the bar. Badinoff isn't bad enough. Richatelli clocks Boris with a couple of undefended rights to the face. Richatelli punches him out and dots his eyes, literally. Badinoff is on the ground with two black eyes and a concussion. He'll miss at least a week. The party ends abruptly. One of the booster club guys, who is also an Icemen employee, volunteers to get Badinoff home in a cab. He rides with him. Richatelli has his right hand in an ice bucket as I leave.

Saturday, December 28

We have two more road games to close out first half of schedule: at Highland on December 30 and then New Year's Eve in Springfield.

Bus for Highland leaves at 2:00 p.m. today (again leaving after twelve noon so owner doesn't have to pay the players a lunch per diem). Highland is a good twelve-hour run, and the boys are still dusty from the party the night before. But we have a light skate this morning, work out some of the alcohol. They can sleep on the bus. There should be some extra room, too, since Badinoff (concussion) and Richatelli (dinged-up right hand) are not on the trip. Both will miss the next two games.

After the skate, we go to put our bags on the bus. In the loading dock with my bag, I literally say out loud, "What the fuck?" Our normal luxury coach-style bus the Icemen always travel in is nowhere to be seen. I'm looking at a yellow school bus, all beat to shit and with three inches of exhaust soot across the backside. It really is an old-school bus! Yes, it has the required fourteen rows of seats. But they are nonreclining, straight-up seat backs. And *no toilet*!

I whip out my cell and call GM Lakor to tell him there must be a mistake. We are going to travel almost thirty hours in the next couple of days in this gas station dumpster on wheels. It's all about the Benjamins. "Much cheaper than the luxury, coach," I'm told by Lakor. "Play better. You'll get a better bus." Lakor hangs up. Conversation over. I hate cost control.

The bus is disgusting. Slade says it smells like a cabdriver's ass. I'll take his word for it. (That's one of those comments that suddenly make you an expert. Do you *know* what a cabbie's ass smells like? Kinda like "Have you ever smelled moth balls? How did you get their tiny legs apart?")

Did I mention there is no bathroom on the bus? To take a piss, we are supposed to use a long-necked yellow plastic funnel strategically inserted through the door weather stripping. Step down into the bus stairwell and let it fly into the funnel. There is no shitter on the bus for a twelve-hour trip to Highland, four hours to Springfield, then another twelve back to Charlestowne.

Randy Beacon from Section 8 and DePasto Olds is our driver. He tries to put a bright face on pissing into a funnel while going down the highway at seventy miles per hour. I tell him to wait until I have to take a dump and leave a big heater in that funnel. Let's see if you smile then.

Rolling down the highway early in the twelve-hour trip, Barnes interrupts the sleeping, video games, and card playing to talk about *why* we are on *this* bus. He really doesn't want to talk about cutting costs to the players. That can boomerang on you. He stammers. Finally, Barnes reaches deep down inside to fire off a Winston Churchill motivational quote: *If you're going through hell, keep going.* The bus isn't hell yet. But after thirty hours without a shitter on board, its gonna look and smell like a Calcutta sewage treatment plant.

Budler is the first Icemen to step down into the stairwell and take care of number 1. Shortly after he starts to piss, Trainer Chuck notices some drizzle forming on the outside his row-three window. Budler's piss is being pushed by the wind back onto the right side of the bus. How appropriate. We are literally pissing on ourselves.

Beacon seems to be driving slower than normal. The time-honored hockey comment about slow bus drivers is a shouted, loud and clear, from Chrisler, "Hey, bussie. Step on it! There's a dog pissing on your wheel." Timely and situation appropriate!

Monday, December 30 at Highland
Win 4–1

It's a strange schedule. End of December and this is the first time all season we've played the Highland Kilt Lifters. Badinoff and Richatelli are both out. We're short one player. But Chrisler and LeGault step up with a couple of timely goals. Crosby does the rest stopping twenty-nine of thirty shots.

We are headed to Springfield after the game on the bus the boys are now calling the Iron Lung. They're also still shaking their heads over the incident from Friday night's team Christmas party. It'll be interesting to see how they treat Badinoff when he returns. Richatelli is fine, defending the family honor and all that. The other kid is a nineteen-year-old Russian superstar who is going to be an NHL goal scoring champ. That's something none of these Icemen will ever be.

Tuesday, December 31 at Springfield
Win 5–3

New Year's Eve. Time to appreciate the good things from the past year and leave the bad ones behind. It's been mostly bad ones so far this season for the Icemen, their fans, and the City of Charlestowne (greedy, crooked civic and mafia types not included).

Icemen close out the first half of their last season with a 5–3 road win. That puts our final December record at 7-4-1, including four wins in a row now. We have as many wins this month as we did October-November combined. The team is coming around. Just hope the hole we dug over the first twenty-four games didn't end up burying us.

The team has a quiet New Year's Eve (NYE) celebration back at the Marriott. Hotel is nice enough to hold a ballroom for us, catered with postgame meal and some beer. No one is saying much except for Crosby who is really coming out of his shell. The Professor wins again tonight. But the Badinoff/Richatelli dust up is still on everyone's mind and puts a damper on the win and the evening.

In the ballroom next door, there is a *loud* NYE party in full Happy New Year swing. As our party starts to break up, a couple of the players crash the party next door. I see DeMarko and Lombardozzi hustle a hottie out of there. The three of them make their way arm in arm to the elevator bank. Looks like those tunnel buddies are back in business or as they would call it, "Ripken time."

CHAPTER 5

Bikini Night, Grand Theft Auto, and the Hockey Sex Glossary

Wednesday, January 1

It is a day to reflect quietly on friends, family, football, and the first half. A decent December put the Icemen at 14-19-3 at the turn, thirty-one points out of a possible seventy-two. At that rate, we won't get it done. We won't make the playoffs with sixty-two points. My guess is we'll need to be in the mid to high seventies to finish in top four Eastern division. Right now, we sit eleven points out of that final playoff spot. Is the Icemen's last season going to be one of the worst in their thirty-eight-year history?

New Year's Day used to be the best day of the year for college football. Not anymore. Today's TV schedule filled with tier-two-quality bowl games. I get to watch Michigan lose again. I agreed with getting rid of Harbaugh years ago, but Coach Isanhart needs to make this an elite program again.

Thursday, January 2

Let's start out the New Year with a *bang*, literally. Unedited for adult entertainment purposes only (please no wagering), and on behalf of all male hockey players, I'm pleased to present *Icemen hockey insider lesson of the month.* This month's lesson: the hockey sex glossary.

There's an old saying that whoever wins the war gets to write the history. This glossary of hockey sex terms is kind of like that, written from one side. As I enlighten you with this knowledge, you'll no doubt come to realize (and appreciate) that this hockey sex glossary is written by men. The sheer number of slang for male genitalia and masturbation versus the number for women should be a dead giveaway.

Without further ado, hockey sex glossary 101.

(1) *The female spectrum.*

Before we take the tour, a couple of standard ground rules.

Teammate's family members are out of bounds. Do not touch. Badinoff broke the code here, and the result was two black eyes and a concussion. This rule extends beyond immediate family and sisters. Even cousins are off-limits unless you have expressed written consent from your teammate. Text or email will suffice.

Expressed written consent from your teammate is required to plow his ex-wife. Text or email will again suffice.

No permission of any kind is required from a teammate to bang his ex-girlfriend but please, be sensitive about how long they have been broken up. Man code says you run some risks on anything less than forty-eight hours.

With that out of the way, players break down the female species into five pedigrees ranked from bottom to top.

Jailbait females under the legal age in that state (or province) to engage in sexual relations. Need to avoid this classification at all costs and for obvious reasons. Close rate should be 0 percent.

Players who chase jailbait will hear from teammates comments like "Hey, bud! Let the paint dry, eh?" and "No grass on the infield, no play ball." (This still works in Europe but is complicated in North America.)

Several years ago, the Icemen had a vice president busted by the FBI for having kiddie porn on his work computer. Other front office employees where shocked since the man had two small kids of his own. They were suspicious something was up though. Right before the VP's work computer was seized by the FBI. Icemen HR and arena security types distracted others working that day with small-talk blather. It is very unusual that those people would have a fifteen-minute generic conversation with you unless trying to divert your attention.

Rippers (also known as peelers or stripers). Every well-adjusted male at some point in his life while in a strip club has said out loud to his buddies, "No, this is different. She really likes me for me. I think there is something going on here." What's going on is twenty-dollar bills flying out of your wallet one song at a time. Close rate is 30 percent.

There have been more than a few hockey players who dated a ripper. But those relationships last about as long as Britney Spears's first marriage.

Puck bunny (most prevalent of the species). No one has ever been able to catalogue the total number of subspecies. The main difference between a puck bunny and a ripper is simple: The puck bunny seeks you out. Hockey players always have to go to the ripper's lair to engage. Outside that, there is not a lot of difference. Both will cost you some dollars, drinks if nothing else for the puck bunny. Close rate is 85 percent.

The most common nesting areas are bars inside the actual arena, sports bars within a five-mile radius of the arena and any bar where the players hang out.

Rockets (the Ferrari of the species, exotic style combined with drop-dead gorgeous). They are hot, sexy, and flashy all in one package. They are built for speeding through dangerous curves. Her large twin turbos are sometimes factory standard but most likely aftermarket.

But who cares? Close rate is only 50 percent because a rocket knows she's a rocket. She's got other options in the room besides hockey players. If you get to test drive a rocket, try to keep your escape velocity over ninety seconds. Good luck.

Snipe (also known as a snipey). This is a rocket plus, Lamborghini level. The ultimate hottie never comes cheap. In fact, a snipe is out of

the range of most AHA hockey players. A snipe almost always wants
to be ridden by an NHLer or NBA.

(2) *Terminology.*

The hockey slang dictionary for common sex terms.

Intercourse. Throwing hip, banging uglies, take down, toe
curler, clam slammer, bury the salami, the old in-out, plow, laying
pipe (especially popular in Alberta), impale, ride the baloney pony,
the horizontal mambo, beef injection, spear, harpoon (with the fatter ladies), hide the weasel, play a little game called just the tip, and
smash.

Sex/other. Yodeling in the gully (oral), two in the pink, one in
the stink (the shocker), two in the slit, one in the shit (the shocker),
the Weber (Named after hall of fame bowler Dick Weber. Your thumb
in her ass, two fingers in the vagina, like a bowling-ball grip), dance
the chocolate cha-cha (anal), driving the Hershey highway (anal),
riding the dirt trail (anal), and Montana muzzle loader.

Penis. Bobby dangler, chutney ferret, custard slinger, dink,
disco stick, friendly weapon, ground squirrel, hard drive / floppy
disk, hollow point, horn, Vlad the Impaler, joystick, middle stump,
PhD, sticky grenade, pork sword, weapon of mass destruction, Uncle
Charley, pipe, man meat, swingin' sirloin, tube steak, vein-laden
meat pipe, and third leg.

Vagina. Box, furry cup, snapper, front bum, kitty cat, mitt, bea-
ver, the gully, clam, and taco.

Male masturbation. Batching (from mixing a batch), beating
the bishop, dishonorable discharge, distributing free literature, feeding the ducks, feeding the geese, firing wristers, hand-to-gland combat, making a bald man puke, playing five-on-one, playing one-man
couch hockey in the dark, pulling your horn, extracting the cataract
from the one-eyed trouser lizard, spanking the monkey, flogging the
hog, and pounding the pud.

Female masturbation. Flicking the bean, diddle, face washing
the little man in the boat, and going Amish (no battery-operated
toys).

Coming up. February's *Icemen hockey insider lesson of the month*: science of the hockey fight.

Friday, January 3

LeGault's smoke booth needs more attention. The broken glass is fixed from before, but his stool is missing now. LeGault thinks it's a vast OAMC conspiracy. I think someone borrowed that stool for another immediate need and forgot to return it. He'll have to stand and smoke for now.

Saturday, January 4
Home versus Highland
Lose 5–2

Starting the second half with back-to-back home games versus Highland saves the Kilt Lifters travel expenses to make one trip and play back-to-back games in our barn instead of making two separate trips.

It is not a good way to start the New Year for the team or for Keeb Chrisler. The Elf started growing a mustache back in November, part of that Movember charity project. Men grow mustaches in November, collect pledges, and the money raised goes to support causes like men's prostate cancer, men's nut cancer, and men's mental health—all very worthy causes.

So Keeb keeps growing his mustache all the way through December. When the New Year hit, he is proudly sporting a full neatly trimmed moustache that does not extend beyond his lips—a classic porn mustache! The porn 'stache being forever immortalized by the Mount Rushmore of male porn stars: Harry Reems, Sasha Gabor, John Holmes, and the George Washington of male porn stars, Ron Jeremy.

For Chrisler's first shift tonight, early first period, he lines up to take a face-off with the Kilt Lifters' Kerry Pouge. Pouge takes one look at Keeb's lip sweater and shakes his head from side to side. "Elf, you *cannot* have a porn 'stache if you're four foot two. It does not work."

Sunday, January 5
Home versus Highland
Win 4–3

We split the back-to-back games with Highland. Chrisler and his porn 'stache play a great game. He has two assists and leads the team in a zero for six PK on the Kilt Lifters. We go on the road for five of the next six games, which could make or break our season.

This long road is partially due to Olympia Arena hosting an exhibition by the Chinese national gymnastics team on January 11–12. In an effort to help lagging gymnastics ticket sales, the Icemen allowed one of the female Chinese gymnasts to play Shoot the Puck after the first period tonight. She gets one shot at the far net from center ice. The net is covered with a board. At the bottom of the board is a hole *just* big enough for a puck to get through. Put the puck completely through the hole, and you win a brand-new SUV from DePasto Oldsmobile.

This little 4'8" gymnast speaks no English. I'm sure she has never held a hockey stick. She takes a whack at the puck, reminiscent of a farmer trying to kill a snake with a stick. Shot has plenty of steam, but puck is wide left and off target. Suddenly, it hits a rut in the ice, flips up on its edge, and starts to curve toward the net. I'll be damned if that rolling puck doesn't hit the hole *but goes only halfway through*. It stops on the goal line, half over the line and the other half not.

Now the rules (and the insurance policy against someone winning a new SUV) *clearly* states that the puck has to go *all the way* through the opening to win. Half across the line half on the line does not count. Try telling that to the Chinese national gymnastics team. A translator informs the girl she's won a new American SUV from DePasto Oldsmobile. Her coach thinks the SUV should be property of the state and is trying to figure out how to get it back to China. Meanwhile, Mr. DePasto is at the game tonight. He's shaking his head no and waving his arms back and forth like a football referee signaling no good on a field goal attempt.

Once it becomes clear the gymnast will not get the SUV (rules are rules), the crowd starts to boo and rain debris on the ice. The coach of the Chinese national gymnastics team is livid and threatens to pull the plug on the November 11–12 event at Olympia Arena. Jimmy Bozatoni, the arena's marketing guy who arranged the shoot the puck to help pump gymnastics ticket sales, is irate. He blames the Icemen management. Bozatoni claims its political payback from the Icemen.

Don't forget the Chinese government is providing a large chunk of the financing for the new arena through the federal EB-5 program. (Give Uncle Sam money for projects he can't afford to do on his own anymore, and the US will give you immigration visas up the yin-yang.) Beijing doesn't like to see their Olympic gymnastics team embarrassed. The Chinese ambassador to the United States is personally blowing up Mayor Vizzyello's cell phone.

Wednesday, January 8

The boys are having a few beers in the hotel bar the night before playing Great Lakes. Famous for their atomic wings, the bar not only discourages you from ordering them, they'll make you sign a binding legal waiver before serving you. The waiver says you release the bar from all claims, warns you to not share wings with anyone else, eat them only in the bar, don't touch your face while eating them, wash your hands immediately afterward, etc.

Steele is crazy enough to try atomic wings. He's still dressed in his workout clothes. The boys bait him and bet cash money he can't eat the whole serving. The wings show up. There are only four, but as soon as the waitress (wearing a mask and gloves BTW) sets them down, the fumes start to overtake the table: ghost peppers, cayenne, Da Bomb hot sauce, and probably kerosene! The wagers against Steele grow quickly—pisses him off even more. A couple of the vets try and talk him out of it. Fuck, we need him to play tomorrow night, not be hospitalized.

Steele utilizes a knife, fork, and dipping the wings in fromunda cheese. He eats all four atomic wings. He fires them down as quick as he can before the heat and sting get to be too much. Triple-6 is counting his winnings (152.00 dollars) and sweating his ass off. He's mumbling incoherently, and his complexion is turning from orange to white back to orange. More milk is not putting out the fire in his stomach. Eating quick may have been a good strategy to win the bet. But ten minutes later, his organs are taking an ass beating.

Steele's face suddenly contorts, and his stomach lets out a long, low, aching rumble unlike anything I have ever heard in my life. The fire has dropped to his colon. Steele needs to act now because those atomic wings are going to burn a hole all the way through him. He stands up and moves quickly into the bar bathroom. He is out just as quickly. The stall is occupied. Steele goes up to a waitress. Barely holding his shit together, Steele asks her where the closest bathroom is outside the bar. She points across the hotel lobby, all the way across—a good forty yards. Steele has no choice. He needs to make a run across the lobby. The atomic wings are eating *him* up now—teeth clenched, pale white, sweaty, hunched over, and ass cheeks pinched together as well I'll bet. Steele sets sail for the lobby bathroom.

All of us have experienced the shits, diarrhea, or Montezuma's revenge. The clenched-ass-cheeks strategy works okay if you are sitting down. But once you are upright, moving your legs, and trying to sprint across a hotel lobby, all bets are off. Steele isn't fifteen yards out of the bar when he springs a leak. Dark-brown liquid from underneath his shorts is running down the back of his legs. His seat has a spreading wetness on it with every step he takes. Halfway across, Steele loses all hope of holding anything in. The shit flow is a steady stream now. Steele is kicking up shit with his shoes as he runs, like sprinting through a mud bog. The spray is leaving a pattern on the back of his shirt and in his hair. Steele is now across the lobby and into the bathroom. But the damage is done. There is a shit trail from the bar twenty-five yards long across the lobby. It grows in intensity, volume, and darkness as you look across the marble lobby floor. The hotel workers at the front desk are mortified. A cleaning woman with a simple mop and bucket appears. The look on her face is one of utter agony and gloom, like she is staring at Satan himself.

LeGault's cell phone rings. Steele is calling from the lobby shitter and asks his roomie to please bring him a change of clothes from the hotel room. Steele's social media fails to cover this event.

Thursday, January 9 at Great Lakes
Lose 4–0

Petr Orelik shuts us out. We are never in it. It is over faster than the musical career of Flock of Seagulls. At least those guys had one hit. We don't touch anyone tonight. Storm players never break a sweat. We put out zero effort. Neither team needs a postgame shower.

Orelik stones fellow countryman Badinoff twice on breakaways. That is as close as we came to a goal. Badinoff has not said boo to anyone since returning from the beatdown Richatelli gave him December 27. I'm a little worried. I'm Gonna ask Dr. Modato to talk to Boris.

Saturday, January 11 at Michigan
Lose 6–3

I do like playing in Detroit, but I'm in a bad mood before the game. I'm still chaffing from that shit show two nights ago against Great Lakes.

This one doesn't go much better for the Icemen. By the third period, I'm really steaming, embarrassed that my friends and family have to watch this. The Command's Andy Davis has been chirping all night, and about nine minutes into the third, I've had enough. Al's a middleweight like me, so I'm not breaking any code. I want to fight him. I run Davis from behind hard into the end glass. Ref's hand goes up. I'm getting a minor for charging. I might as well get my monies' worth. I drop the gloves and poke Davis a couple of times to get him to go. He drops his gloves, and he starts to throw. Davis catches me with a left hook. My knees buckle, and I've got those squiggly things dancing in both eyes, seeing stars you civilians might call it. I'm wounded and going down. Before I hit the ice, I load up one big right hand and just fire it off blindly. It catches Davis right in the Chiclets hard. We both hit the ice—fight over.

I'll be in penalty box for seven minutes. My right hand is killing me. I might have broken it. After a couple of minutes in the ice bucket, I pull my hand out to examine. Between my index finger and the middle finger, I see two of Al's teeth embedded in my knuckles.

Monday, January 13

Pittinger goes back on the DL today. Whirlpool is suffering from blurry, burning eyes and having trouble focusing. Cooking Mexican food Sunday night, he failed to wash his hands after handling raw ghost peppers and rubbed his eyes. For the next week, Pitt will use eye-drop medication and wear a patch over the right eye.

Boomer strikes again. Before practice ends, he gets into the locker room early and saran wraps the shitter in stall number 3. He's done this before. Boomer knows for maximum effect, the clear saran wrap *must* be placed between the seat and the bowl itself. If you drape the saran wrap over the seat, yes, it's still hard to see. But you run a real risk of the shitter sitting on it before they drop a deuce and realizing what's up.

Precisely placed and trimmed between the bottom of the seat and the bowl, Crosby has no chance. He takes a nasty anthill-style dump, but the saran keeps it from hitting the water. Faster than Crosby could scream, "FUCK! BOOMER! FOR FUCK'S SAKES!" his ass is covered in his own shit. Ditto for his underwear and shower shoes, they get hit by the overflow onto the floor. Boomer has the whole thing on video from outside the stall, of course. Twitter literally loves this shit.

Tuesday, January 14
Home versus Peninsula
Win 7–2

Craigsen continues to do his best Lazarus impersonation. Had 2/2 tonight for four points. Big win, and everyone gets a free small french fry from Bumpa's Burgers.

Icemen marketing ran one of our biggest promotions of the year tonight, the annual Bikini Night. Bikini night always moves a lot of tickets. A Tuesday game in mid-January needs all the help it can get. Fans register ahead of time and walk across a carpet on the ice during intermission, wearing their bikinis. A group of celebrity judges picks the winners based on crowd reaction as contestants are introduced one at a time. The ultimate winner gets a trip for two to see Icemen play at Peninsula on March 26.

Bikini night has been a lynchpin on the Icemen marketing calendar for several years. Most of us assume the female participants who sign up are all girl-next-door hockey fans. (Male contestants were eliminated a few years ago because the crowd would boo and throw food at them as they walked across the ice.) Turns out most of the rockets are imports from the legendary Charlestowne strip joint Backdoor Jimmy's. Jimmy has provided six to eight of the contestants every year.

Celebrity judges are traditionally made up of Icemen alumni and local media talent. Mr. Hockey is blessing everyone with his presence as a celebrity judge tonight. The bikini contest round 1 during the first intermission goes flawlessly. Second intermission is for the finalists and to pick a winner of the trip. Right before the girls go back out for the finals, Mr. Hockey starts a small riot backstage when he grabs a handful of one of the contestants. Her name is Tiffany, maybe a stage name. Who knows? Who cares? The one thing about Tiffany we know for sure: She is one of Backdoor Jimmy's all-stars. Jimmy and the chaperons assigned to watch over his girls are pissed. Mr. Hockey gets two DD-size handfuls, and before he can get the third squeeze in, chaperones and Icemen alumni are colliding. The arena has a couple of security people there, too, to keep gawking fans away

111

from the contestants, not to protect them from Mr. Hockey. Lots of shouting, pushing, and shoving. But no punches. The Icemen's last Bikini Night will certainly be one of its more memorable!

Tiffany comes in second in the finals. Mr. Hockey gets the crowd going and funnels their cheers behind Anastasia. She wins the trip. Tiffany wins second. Paris gets the bronze for third.

Wednesday, January 15

GM Lakor makes a huge move today. Somehow, he works his magic and grabs Highland defenseman Jon Sanderson in a waiver deal. Sanderson is a veteran, perennial all-star-caliber player in the Western division. Kilt Lifters are going nowhere this season, so they move Sandy as a favor to him. Sanderson's nickname is Machine. He never makes a mistake at either end of the ice. He'll automatically be our number 2 defenseman after LeGault.

This is great news for everyone but Pittinger. Lakor and Barnes are tired of Pitt being injured, and if the Icemen are going to make a run, we need high-quality D we can count on.

Thursday, January 16 at Gotham
Lose 2–1

Sanderson is here in time to make the early bus to Gotham for tonight's game. We know each other a bit but not a ton, playing in different divisions all these years. I know he's from British Columbia and quite the surfer, legend has it. I'll spend some quality time with him later. I greet Machine as he is throwing his equipment bag into the bus cargo hold. He greets me a "'Sup, Han Brolo!" Hammer walks by. Sanderson goes into a bicep-muscle flex, points at Hammer, and blurts out, "Hey, Guns N' Broses."

Machine says he's excited to here but "gonna miss steak-and-blow-job day." I guess his nineteen-year-old girlfriend picks a random day several times a month and declares it steak-and-blow-job day. Lucky bastard. I like steak.

We lose a hard-fought game to the Metros, and Hawkes loses a fight to Scott Cirvelloe. Cirvelloe is a lefty, and Hawkes doesn't know that. He sets up to fight a right-hander when they square off. The Gotham vet feeds Hawkes a huge left and hit the kid square on the beak. Down goes Hawkes! Down goes Hawkes! That'll be part of next month's *Icemen insider hockey lesson: science of the hockey fight.* Item number 1: Before you throw, know which way the other guy goes.

I fought Cirvelloe three seasons ago. That fucker earholed me. Cirvelloe hit me so hard with that left, he spun my helmet around, and I was looking through the right earhole, hanging on for dear life. I did not win that one.

Friday, January 17

Bus to Cleveland. Chuck, Sal, and DeMarko switch their seats around, trying to change the road karma. Chuck ends up behind me. He asks what hotel we are staying at, and I tell him the DoubleTree. We immediately go down memory lane when Chuck and I would room together on the road.

About ten years ago in Cleveland, we stayed at the DoubleTree the night before our game against the Steamers. The Cavaliers played that night. When the game was over, Chuck and I went out on the balcony to watch the fans streaming to their cars. The game hadn't been over ten minutes. And there's LeBron, fully dressed and working his way down the street. There's no way he showered. The game had been over only ten minutes! Chuck and I were watching LeBron and doing a point/counterpoint.

"Shower or no shower?"

Suddenly, Chuck starts to scream at LeBron from the fourth-floor balcony, "Hey, stinky! Hey, LeBron! What the fuck? No shower for you? Hey, LeBron! You hiding something? Embarrassed about something you don't want your teammates to see, like a little dick? Or maybe you just enjoy being a stank-ass Cleveland piece of shit? Hey, stank ass! Hey, stinky LeBron."

I don't know if LeBron heard Chuck, but it made me laugh that night. And again today.

Saturday, January 18 at Cleveland
Lose 5–0

Guess who was stank ass tonight? That would be your Charlestowne Icemen. It is Bill Ennet (not to be confused with brother Bob, also a goalie) with the shutout. We look tired, third game in four days, last two on the road. Cleveland's Jack Chandler is a year older than me. We grew up in the same Detroit neighborhood, only a couple of streets apart actually. He skates up to me after a whistle.

Chandler, smiling, says, "Fuck, Vito. You look OLD."

I, smiling back, say, "We were old ten years ago."

Chandler, skating away, says, "Can you believe we're this fucking old, still playing this fucking game?"

Monday, January 20

Pittinger thinks he'll be released with Sanderson now here. Craigsen convinces Pitt to go see Dr. Modato. He tells Pitt how much Modato has helped him, getting his game back on track. Pittinger better do something. He's likely back in the lineup tomorrow after missing one week due to the ghost-pepper incident. He's also still on Barnes's shit list. It's fifty-fifty whether we keep Pitt.

Tuesday, January 21 at Tri-Cities
Win 4–2

Pittinger is back in the lineup and plays pretty well. He has one assist and goes plus two. He almost has a goal, too, on the power play. Danny Fumay makes a crazy save on a Pittinger slapper from close in.

Thursday, January 23

Win a game, and the players think it's okay to fuck around with Coach Barnes's pride and joy. The boys have his car towed during our morning practice. It is towed but stored safely at the Charlestowne PD impound. CPD was in on this one from the start.

Now this isn't any car. This is a motherfucking classic: a vintage, tricked-out mint 1975 baby-blue Corvette T-top. It underwent a frame-off restoration a couple of years ago, and Barnes dropped about fifty thousand dollars on the engine as well. The 1975 Chevrolet Corvette Pro Touring came with the standard 350 LT1. Barnes had it bored out to a 390 kicking out almost four hundred horsepower. He installed Edelbrock performer heads, hooker headers, MSD ignition, and a Holley racing carb. The tranny is a fully rebuilt Turbo 400 4-speed B+M 2400 Stall. All engine components are chrome, even the water pump and radiator. Stainless-steel side pipes (aka ankle burners) are the cherry on top.

Barnes goes to leave after practice. He sees his car has been stolen. He doesn't initially think the players did it. That morning, Barnes was running late for practice and didn't park in our assigned lot. Instead, he pulled right up to the loading dock and grabbed a handicapped spot. Barnes thinks Vinnie Esposito, the Olympia Arena ops guy, had it towed for being illegally parked. Barnes snaps. He goes down to Esposito's office on the other side of the arena's lower level and proceeds to thrash it. He's turning over desks and tables, punching file cabinets and sweeping stuff off Esposito's desk. All the time, Espo has this stunned look and keeps asking, "What car? What the fuck are you talking about?" and "Don't break that! My kids made it!" Too late.

Barnes finds out later that a couple of the players (Fuck! Boomer! For fuck's sakes!) were behind it. But he won't apologize to Esposito. Barnes figures its payback for putting the Icemen out of business.

Friday, January 24
Home versus Cleveland
Lose 5–3

What a shit show. The game is delayed for two hours right before the start. Our mascot gets his jersey caught in the repelling equipment as he tries to descend as part of the pregame ceremony. The mascot gets snagged and just hangs there, thirty feet above the ice, until the Charlestowne Fire Department arrives with a cherry picker.

Instead of a 7:05 p.m. puck drop, we didn't get going until 9:00 p.m. But the good folks at OAMC keeps selling beer during the delay. Everyone is good and shit-faced when the game starts. When it ends, they are fall-down puke on your own shoes drunk. I hear afterward it was a new record for beer sales at an Icemen regular season game. The Arena Club will be hand-to-hand combat tonight. Frankie Cal better keep that twelve-gauge within arm's length.

Monday, January 27

Bus to North Jersey. There is no Hammer on this trip. It's the last game of his suspension from that December bench clearer. Hawkes and Steele will have their hands full with House Painter goons like Bill Hunter and that mouth-breathing ginger, Becker.

I'm sitting across from Sal, the equipment guy. He's got his tablet out and binging on the TV show *Ridiculousness*. That show is fantastic. I watch out of the corner of my eye. Lombardozzi notices and angles the tablet screen toward me a bit so I can see better. Sal knows I love Rob Dyrdek. I love Chanel West Coast even more. She's one of my one-month girls.

Tuesday, January 28 at North Jersey
Lose 4–3

We lose a hard-fought game 4–3. Tons of fights. Steele has three and gets an automatic game misconduct for that. He is gone early in the third period. Triple-6 handles his own with Becker who is a fucking beast. That does not go unnoticed.

DeMarko tonight goes through every one of his slang for fight—rag dolled, jelly-legged, starched, filled in. He even breaks out the Irish handshake after Seamus O'Malley headbutts Chrisler in a scuffle.

Friday, January 31 at Elmdale
Win 5–0

Barnes plays a hunch and starts Zeleski between the pipes. Z-man gets a thirty-two-shot shutout. Barnes is lucky gambling on his goalies at this point in the playoff race. If Zeleski had lost, there would have been more second-guessing than schizophrenic's week on *Jeopardy!* (Miss ya, Alex.)

Craigsen, Libbet, Hightower, Budler, and Badinoff get a goal each. All three lines play well. Sanderson is making a big difference on D.

The Elmos have a Hanson brothers promo tonight. The three stars from the all-time greatest hockey movie ever, *Slap Shot*, are here signing autographs. They are also a big part of tonight's in-game entertainment. I see Dave Hanson after warm-up in the back of the house. He's headed out soon to drop the ceremonial first puck. I know Dave very well. I know his kid, Christian, a bit, too, when he broke into the pros. I only have a couple of minutes with Dave, and we haven't seen each other in quite a few years. As it is with any good friend, though, you never miss a beat. It feels like the last time we caught up was just last week.

Almost five decades after the release of *Slap Shot*, Dave and the two Carlsons, Jeff and Steve, are still making money on it. God bless them. Dave and I hug goodbye. I walk toward our locker room. Dave yells at me in that Hanson brothers' voice, "OLD TIME HOCKEY, EH?" I love that guy.

CHAPTER 6

Hat Tricks, Horsemen, and the Road Trip from Hell

Sunday, February 2
Home versus Wilson Falls
Win 4–2

It is the first time we've seen the Driftwoods since playing them twice in October. We won both of those games, scored six goals each time. Not tonight. The Driftys show some pride. Icemen win again but need an empty net goal by Sanderson to put it away. He's been a huge addition to the team, given us a real shot of confidence. All Machine does tonight is get the ENG to wrap up the win for Crosby. He is also plus three.

Afterward, I get a group of the veterans organized to have dinner with Sanderson Tuesday night. We haven't had time to properly welcome him to the team: Libbet, Hightower, Slade, Bradberry, LeGault, and me. Sandy makes seven. I tell him the plan. Machine says, "Cool! Thanks, Brobi-Wan Kenobi."

Tuesday, February 4

It is dinner for the lucky seven tonight. We skip the Backcheck Lounge and Richatelli's Sports Bar. Captain Libbet and I lead a group of four other Icemen veterans and treat Sanderson to a classy Charlestowne eatery, Carmine's Steak and Chop House—not cheap. Good thing we can split the tab six ways.

Six bottles of wine into the evening, and Machine is talking about surfing off the British Columbia coast. Sanderson is a BC surf bum. He grew up in Tofino, a small town located on the west coast of Vancouver Island. He was born there, raised there, and makes his off-season home there. Sandy says he doesn't surf as much as he did as a kid but is still very active when his hockey season ends. Tofino has twenty-two miles of surfable beach break. If you want to know about hanging ten at Cox Bay, North or South Chesterman beaches, then Sandy is your surf sherpa.

Steaks are great, wine is better, and Sanderson is the best. He's fucking hilarious. I ask him how many variations of bro he has in his vocabulary. He's been with us almost three weeks now, and I've never heard him use the same bro twice. Slade bets him twenty dollars he can't go the rest of night talking to us and restaurant staff without running out of bros.

Machine explains bro talk started years ago with his BC surfer buddies. They try and one up each other with a new broism all the time. Looking at Slade, barely taking a breath, Sanderson rattles off, "Abroham Lincoln, Albert PuBrols, Angelina Brolie, Axl Brose, Bro Jackson, Bro Montana, Bro Peche, Bro J Simpson, Broba Fett, Brobi-Wan Kenobi, Brobocop, Brocahontas, Brohammad Ali, Brohan Solo, Brohemian, Broprah Winfrey, Brorannasaurs Rex, Brosa Parks, Broseph, Broseph Stalin, Brosideon, Brosie O'Donnell, Broski, brotato chip, brotein shake, brovolone cheese, Brozo the Clown, C-3PBro, Dikembe Mutumbro, GI Bro, Guns N' Broses, Han Brolo, Hulk Brogan, Joe Brogan, Kimbro Slice, Kurt Brobain, Lindsey Brohan, Marilyn Monbro, REBro Speedwagon, Ringbro Starr, Robert Denirbro, RobroCop, Rocky Balbroa, Russel Bro, Sandy Broufax, Scarlett Brohansson, Seth Brogan, Shaquille Bro'neil, Sheryl Bro, Sonny Brono, Teddy Broosevelt, the Big Brobowski, Tim Tebrow, Vincent Van Brogh, the Brope, leader of the Broman Catholic Church, Nabroleon Dynamite, Evander Brolyfield, and Tony Bromo."

That's almost sixty bros in under two minutes. Still looking at Slade, Machine says, "Keep the twenty dollars, Evil Bro Slade. Put it toward post-dinner cigars." The table erupts with laugher. Machine is fitting in just fine.

Wednesday, February 5 at Highland
Win 6–2

We lifted their kilts and kicked their asses. We're scoring goals in bunches suddenly. Tonight's six make it fifteen goals in the last three games. With that kind of scoring, either Crosby or Zeleski should be fine.

Hawkes and Highland's Neal Desoremo are both given game misconducts after an exceptionally ugly fight late second period. Desoremo trash-talks Hawkes every time they are on the ice together. Hawkes keeps his composure and doesn't say a word.

Frustrated that he isn't rattling the rookie, Desoremo says to Hawkes, "What's the problem, rook? You scared? Or deaf. Maybe both." Hawkes turns and looks at Desoremo.

"Sorry, I don't speak cement."

Gloves are off and it is on.

There's a tunnel alongside the visitor's bench in Highland that leads straight back to the visitors' locker room. Kilt Lifters' home bench is on the same side of the rink as the visitors. They have a tunnel, too, back to their locker room. Upon ejection, Hawkes goes down his tunnel, and Desoremo does the same. Everyone thinks the fight is over. There are two tunnels, but they intersect and end at the same hallway. The only thing in that hallway separating the two locker rooms is a flimsy pipe and drape setup guarded by a seventy-year-old part-time arena employee.

We could hear the noise from the bench when Hawkes and Desoremo restart their brawl: steel pipe crashing onto concrete, tables getting overturned, and people screaming and swearing. The seventy-year-old arena employee is literally trampled trying to step between two pissed-off hockey heavyweights. That old fuck is lucky he doesn't get stepped on by a skate blade. The trainers and equipment guys from both teams peel off the bench and race down their respective tunnels. So do a few security guards in the vicinity of the benches. Players can hear everything. We know what's going on in the hallway. But there is also a game underway. Let the other guys break it up.

Thursday, February 6

In the afterglow of last night's classic cage match between Hawkes and Desoremo, this would be ideal placement for the *Icemen hockey insider lesson of the month*: science of the hockey fight.

Early in the season, we talked about The Code, the unwritten set of rules that governs a hockey fight once it starts. But how about the setup—the anatomy of a hockey fight? Building your mechanics and getting in position to win the fight before the punches fly. There is a science to it. But at the end of the day, it is a fistfight. As Mike Tyson famously said, "Everyone has a game plan until they get punched in the mouth."

Science of the hockey fight starts with doing your homework before the game. If there's an opponent you may go with, find out if his main throw is left or right. You *will* want to know this ahead of time. Grabbing the wrong fistful of the others guys' jersey could be hazardous to your health and your teeth.

For this exercise, let's assume both players prefer to throw with their right hands. You both square up in a right-hander's stance.

First, with your left hand, grab a handful of your opponent's jersey, just below his right shoulder. Once your left hand has a firm grip on his jersey, twist it counter clockwise.

Then straighten out your left arm and lock the elbow. Your left arm should be perfectly straight from your shoulder to his right shoulder, no bend at all. This limits your opponent's mobility with his right hand. Keeping your left elbow locked will (hopefully) keep you out of his punching range.

Like your daddy told ya, whether it's a playground scrap or a bar fight, the first punch is key. There are no linesmen in a bar fight. Get the first punch in and make it a good one before buddies on both sides pile on. A hockey fight isn't much different when it comes to the first punch. It won't be over after one punch like most bar fights. But in hockey, that first punch can knock a guy off balance and give you a leverage advantage. That first punch can sting an opponent and let him know he's in for a long bout. Plant that seed of doubt in his mind. Fear may creep in as your opponent asks himself, "Do I really want to do this?"

It's all about your style after that first punch. Whatever works for you. As noted earlier, Hammer's style is over/under and lots of fast punches coming from different angles. Hawkes sits back and lets the other guy tire himself out a bit. His nickname is One Punch for a reason: Hawkes is always looking to land the one big right-hand bomb.

Coming up. March's Icemen hockey insider lesson of the month: keep your poop grouped. That shit is funny.

Saturday, February 8
Home versus Cleveland
Lose 7–4

Craigsen gets a hat trick, but he can't outscore the Steamers by himself. His game and his attitude are *much* better after his Christmas consultation with Dr. Modato. Craigsen is playing himself back to the Show. If he gets there, he better give Doc Modato some love.

Zeleski goes the whole way and takes a pounding. Poor bastard faces fifty-four shots! It's more obvious now than ever. If we're going to go on a playoff run, Crosby, the rookie, will have to carry the load. But is he really a rookie anymore after dressing for fifty games as a pro? Crosby's college team would play twenty-four to twenty-eight games a season, depending on how far they went in the playoffs. We have that many regular season games still to play! Twenty-four! Crosby will end up playing the most games in one season of his young career by a mile. The challenge for Barnes and I is to keep the kid from getting burned out.

Sunday, February 9

Remember that late December trip we took on the school bus with no toilet and thirty hours of windshield time through three cities? Limping back into Charlestowne after those two road games in an iron long that reeked of ass, stale farts, and spoiled cheese, I thought to myself, *Well, Vito, that's as bad a road trip as you'll* ever *go on.* Of course, I was wrong.

This afternoon, we set off on a three-game roadie: Great Lakes Tuesday, then on to Cleveland and Michigan. There are blizzard warnings all around the Great Lakes area, but we decide to make a run for it—not much choice. We race up I-75 trying to beat the storm, get as far as Lexington, Kentucky, and stop. The weather is okay in Lexington, and we could likely make it through that state. At some point, we need to cut over to I-65, but we can't get all the way through Indiana, let alone into Chicago. Lake Michigan, Lake Huron, and Lake Erie are all getting heavy lake-effect blizzards. Roads into the three cities we need to get to (Chicago, Detroit, and Cleveland) are all snowbound, impassable, and closed. National Guard troops are preventing cars from getting on the freeways in that tristate area because they'll get stuck and stranded.

We're stuck in Lexington. We can't continue driving north, just to get stuck in an Indiana snowbank. It would be the fucking Donner party with this group. Who would we eat first to survive? Probably Sal or Chuck. DeMarko has so many diseases, no one wants to go near that man as a meat source. And let's not eat any players yet. But if push comes to shove, we need only one goalie to play.

Okay. Let's get serious. We've been sitting at a Waffle House in Lexington for over six hours now. Lakor and the rest of the hockey staff back in Charlestowne have been working on options.

The roads won't be clear for two to three days so that doesn't work for a game at Great Lakes that starts in thirty-five hours. Lakor makes the call. The bus veers east a bit, and we check into a Cincinnati hotel. It's 11 a.m. on Monday.

Lakor finds a charter company willing to fly in this weather but not for at least another twenty-four hours. They figure by then the storm will be passed and O'Hare should have a couple of runways open. This charter flight will cost over forty thousand dollars and shoot the travel budget all to hell—not what our owner, Triple R, wants in this final season of Icemen existence. But it's the only way to make the game on time and not forfeit to Great Lakes. We need every point in the standings we can get.

The plan is to charter out of Cincinnati on Tuesday at 1:30 p.m., weather and clear runways at O'Hare willing. A two-hour flight puts us on the ground in Chicago around 3:30 p.m., just enough time to get to the arena for a 7:00 p.m. game. We'll have to check in at the hotel after the game.

Barnes brings the team up to speed on the charter flight. He works in this pearl from Winston Churchill: The pessimist sees difficulty in every opportunity. The optimist sees the opportunity in every difficulty.

It suddenly dawns on me. The entire Upper Midwest is frozen over, and I'm going to assume hell is too. While we were fucking around Sunday getting to Kentucky, the Super Bowl was played. And the Detroit Lions, who had not won a championship of any kind since 1957, beat the Las Vegas Raiders in the Super Bowl. The Leos won it all, and I didn't see one second of the game.

Tuesday, February 11 at Great Lakes
Lose 5–4 in overtime

The charter side of the Cincinnati airport is actually across the river in Kentucky. But let's not get into that. We bid adieu to bus driver Randy Beacon. He's gone as far as he can. After getting us and our gear to the airport, Randy will head back to Charlestowne with the bus. We'll have a different bussie for the remainder of the trip to Michigan and Cleveland. You never know what you are going to get in that scenario. We like Randy because he understands what happens on the road stays on the road.

We get to the arena at 5:00 p.m., two hours before game time. A couple of guys are able to catch a thirty-minute power nap in the trainer's room. Not me and I slept very little in the Cincinnati hotel last night. I'm dragging ass. The entire team is beatdown after it took fifty hours to get from Charlestowne to Chicago (via Cincinnati).

Considering all that, we play valiantly. We lose in overtime 5–4 on a bardownski shot by Ed Paskee. Paskee lets a wrister fly from fifteen feet out. The puck hits the very bottom of the crossbar and shoots straight down into the net. I hear the *ding* when the puck hits metal but don't know it is in the net until the light went on. There is no shame losing on a shot like that, not after the road trip from hell.

Hammer has enough energy to give the gears to the Storm's Jess Schultz. Schultz has a huge melon, way out of proportion to the rest of his body. He's got a fucking moose head. It's as big as the grill on a 1950s Buick. Schultz also wears a full visor, which on normal heads we refer to as wearing a fishbowl. Hammer yells at Schultz, slowly skating past our bench, "Jessie! Where did you find an aquarium to fit your fucking head?"

Wednesday, February 12

I can't believe how much snow there is along the road from Chicago to Cleveland. Newcomer Sanderson wants to know about the horsemen and the pony boys. I tell Sanderson the truth: It's all about the size of the man and the size of the man's little man.

The Horsemen Line is made up of Slade, Libbet, and Hightower. They are each six feet or taller and close to two hundred pounds, three of the bigger Icemen. When it comes to cock size, the three are overproportioned. Slade looks like a porn star. Think baby's arm holding an apple. Hightower buys socks in sets of three. Libbet's johnson is so long, it has an elbow.

The Pony Boys—Budler, Chrisler, and Karvaala—are also blessed with oversize swingin' sirloins for their stature. But those three go 5'10", 5'9", and 5'10" respectively. Budler and Karvaala are 180 pounds dripping wet. Chrisler is 170 to start the season, probably closer to 160 pounds at this point in the season.

Sanderson gets it. He understands the humor that goes with spending six months in a locker room with twenty other naked men. "Thanks, brotato chip."

Friday, February 14 at Cleveland
Win 5–1

Crosby plays great. He's the number 1 star of this one. Barnes is doing a nice job spelling Crosby every once in a while with Zeleski. We need to keep the Professor fresh down the stretch.

I don't dress tonight. Both Pittinger and Sanderson are in. I'll dress tomorrow night in Detroit. That works for me. Pitt gets more minutes than usual tonight. He's playing with more confidence, and Barnes is showing more confidence in him, even giving Pitt some special team's ice time. We chalk up another victory for Dr. Modato it looks like. Give Craigsen a helper for encouraging Pitt to talk with the doc.

Before warm-up I sit with Barnes in the coach's office. DeMarko comes in to tape the Icemen insider for his radio pregame show. I listen quietly as DeMarko asks the same old same old keys-to-the-game type of banal questions. My mind wanders back years ago when long-time assistant coach, Barnes, was finally named Icemen head coach. The first question DeMarko ever asked Barnes in an interview was "How does it finally feel to get a head job?" I still laugh at that one. Did I mention that I'm easily amused?

Saturday, February 15 at Michigan
Win 3–1

A full week after the Lions won the Super Bowl, and this town is still drunk. I can't blame them for a second. I would be too. Rumor is the Elwood has never closed for a minute since Super Bowl Sunday. One Lions championship in my lifetime and I missed it. Fuck me.

Crosby wins again—back-to-back games, back-to-back outstanding outings. He's becoming more vocal around his teammates too. You like to see that in a goalie. It's fun to watch Crosby grow as a team leader right before our eyes. Hightower has one of those oh-shit goals again tonight. This time, he victimizes Command rookie defenseman, Don Jennings. That matchup is not fair.

I take a shot off the side of my left ankle early first period on just my fucking second shift! A real stinger. Fuck, that hurts! I'll need to sit out a couple of shifts until the pain goes away, probably miss the rest of the period. I sit at the end of the bench to stay out of the way. I'm parked right next to Zeleski. He's the backup tender tonight. There's a water bottle right in front of Zeleski. I learn over and grab it. Holding the straw just outside my lips, I squeeze the bottle to shoot a stream into my mouth. Holy fuck! *Vodka*! Straight-up Ketel One! No ice. No tonic. No lime.

I stare incredulously at Zeleski. Z-man grins sheepishly, grabs the bottle, and takes a long swig. Zeleski then hands me a different water bottle and puts the vodka one far away from everyone where only he can reach it. He's glassy eyed and half pounded by the end of the first period. I sure as fuck hope he doesn't have to play tonight.

Tuesday, February 18

Barnes gives us Monday off. With that extra rest and a big game looming tomorrow night at home against Gotham, it's a very spirited practice today. Not a lot of drills, Barnes has us scrimmage mostly. There *is* a lot of physicality to the practice, good clean hitting. Some of the guys are practicing too hard, trying to convince Barnes they deserve more ice time.

That's because the trade deadline is next month, and there are a couple of Icemen literally fighting to stay here. No one should have been surprised when it happened. But then hindsight is always twenty-twenty vision. We likely won't keep both Hawkes and Hammer for the stretch run. They are the same player. Halfway through practice, the immovable object meets the unstoppable force.

As I said, it is a physical practice. Hammer and Hawkes have ran into each other a couple of times hard. One time, you could feel the wind go out of Hawkes' *whoosh* when Hammer hits him right in the chest with his shoulder. The next time they collided on this February afternoon, Hammer feels the kid has gotten the stick up on him, cuts Hammer's lip. Hawkes starts to skate away. Hammer throws his gloves and helmet at Hawkes, then stands still, waiting for the kid to come back to him. Hawkes does, and it's go time. Both guys get a couple of shots in before teammates break it up. You don't want your own players injuring each other in practice.

In the locker room, Barnes and I quietly discuss the fight. It wasn't much, but we're in agreement: Hawkes wins in a split decision.

Wednesday, February 19
Home versus Gotham
Win 5–3

I bump into Metros coach, Haynesworth, after the morning skates. I always try and grab a couple of minutes with Dave if I can. You learn something every time. Haynesworth is hockey's Yoda.

We talk briefly about the upcoming Koontz Cup playoffs and who the AHA favorites might be going in. Neither one of us mentions our respective teams. Haynesworth tells one of his stories I have heard before, but never gets old.

Years ago, he was coaching Gotham in a first-round playoff series against Peninsula. They opened at home, so the Gotham game entertainment crew went all out for the opening ceremony: smoke drums, lasers, Harleys, pyro, flash pods, etc. After ten minutes of exploding shit to get the crowd worked up, it was time to play hockey. The problem was the old arena in Gotham was having trouble venting out all that smoke. They started playing hockey anyway. A low fog of smoke and motorcycle exhaust hovered chest high to the players. Haynesworth was livid. He was pointing at his GM and yelling at him. After the first period, Haynsie didn't go near his locker room. He made a beeline to the press box to yell even more at his GM.

Haynesworth said, "Who approved that shit show? My players couldn't breathe from the smoke. Their eyes were watering. Guys are going blind. What the fuck?"

The Metros GM said, "Well, they approved it."

Haynesworth said, "They. Who the fuck are they?"

The Metros GM said, "You know, they."

That's as long as the conversation went. Gotham lost game 1 at home, and Haynsie was pissed. Next morning, the Metros GM got a call from the AHA office. It was Commissioner Steve Archer on the phone.

The commish said, "I'm going to fine your organization five thousand dollars for the smoke incident last night. A formal complaint has been filed with the league office."

The Metros GM said, "I'm not surprised. I was expecting this call. But who exactly from Peninsula turned us in? Who filed the complaint—one of their coaches, their GM, their owner?"

The commish said, "Oh, no. No one from Peninsula complained. Your coach filed the formal complaint."

Haynesworth had turned in his own team. It cost his own owner five large!

Haynesworth is not always so direct. He can be sneaky smart. Craigsen has another hat trick tonight. Postgame Haynesworth is talking about the resurgence of Craigsen since Christmas. Haynsie tells reporters *he* thinks Craigsen is the best offensive player in the AHA right now and that he should be back up in the NHL. Wait! We play Gotham two more times in April. Is Haynesworth setting us up—trying to get Craigsen recalled by his NHL team so we'd need to play two potential playoff impacting games versus the Metros without Craigsen? Sly bastard.

Fans chant, "Hammer. Hammer," throughout the game tonight. It's clear who they want to keep if it comes down to Hammer *or* Hawkes. Section 8 leads the chants. They love Bob. Trade deadline is in less than two weeks.

By the way, that is our first win against Gotham this season after three straight losses—another good sign.

Friday, February 21

"BOOMER! FUCK! BOOMER! FOR FUCK'S SAKES!" Or as they say in Russia, "Нерт возьми! Бумер! Ради всего святого!"

Another timeless classic. Boomtown puts Atomic Balm penetrating heat gel in Badinoff's jock. Atomic Balm is good for muscle soreness—not good in your jock when you're skating around and working up a sweat. It reacts to heat, and the balm starts to burn.

Boris actually has to leave practice and go wash his junk off. It burns so much.

Badinoff is playing much better. He's shaken off the post-holiday blues he went through after the fight with Richatelli over his sister. Boris spent some time with Dr. Modato to get his head back on straight. It's a good sign Boomer picks on him today. The vets feel Boris is back on his game, so they can start fucking with him again.

Modato might be our MVP—most valuable priest. He's gotten Craigsen and Pittinger back on their games and now apparently Badinoff.

Saturday, February 22
Home versus Old Market
Win 9–4

Nine goals tonight for the good guys! Nine in one game! Back in October and Yes-vember, that was a whole week's output. Do the fans get one and a half orders of Bumpa's Burgers fries for nine goals?

That's our first win of the season versus Old Market too. We had lost the previous three to them. We're starting to beat the teams we need to beat. We're crawling back into this playoff race. Gotham and Old Market are in our division. These are four-point games. To win both in regulation, not give up a point in the standings to either foe, is huge.

Don't look now, but so far in February, your Icemen are 6–1. Playoff whispers are heard around the locker room. Just whispers, however. We're still ten points out of the last playoff spot with nineteen games left to play. To quote the Wolf from Pulp Fiction: Now let's not start sucking each other's dicks just yet.

Monday, February 24

I find out Richatelli is working with the Icemen marketing department, brainstorming promotional ideas. I think that's great. This is a player who has his head screwed on right. Tony knows he won't play hockey in the Show. He's preparing for life after hockey. I could see him as a coach in this league one day.

Tuesday, February 25

Nice weather in Dallas, must be over ninety degrees. And no one died falling from a helicopter while hunting wild hogs with .50 calibers. We are already ahead of the game from the previous trip here.

I spoke too soon. We check into hotel on Tuesday for a Wednesday game against Texas. I get a call at 1:00 a.m. from the hotel front desk. Some of our players are jumping off their second-floor balconies and into the pool. Hotel security is knocking on my door. I'm on the seventh floor at the other end of the hotel. This is exactly why on the road, I try and stay as far from the players' rooms as I can.

I follow hotel security down to the second floor, and the boys settle down quickly. Steele is the ringleader on the balcony diving. Crazy fucker.

Wednesday, February 26 at Texas
Lose 4–1

We can't win every game in February. The Icemen embrace that philosophy tonight, losing to the host Marshalls. Texas goalie, Vern Lawler, played well. Badinoff gets our only goal. Greg Whitehorne has two for the winners. And no one died falling from a helicopter while hunting wild hogs with .50 calibers.

Friday, February 28

The AHA trading deadline is March 3, only three days away.

Hawkes and Hammer have another go in practice today. The outcome this time is devastating for Bob. Hawkes won a close decision in their practice fight ten days ago. He honored the code: You always owe the other guy a rematch. Today, Lufthammer gets his.

Hawkes is ready this time to fight a teammate in practice. The two heavies dance for a bit. Hammer tries the over/under on Hawkes. Then One Punch lives up to his nickname. A big right hand, and down goes Hammer. Barnes and I look at each other. GM Lakor is at practice. We shoot him a glance. He nods yes at us. Lakor sees what we do. Hawkes pulled that punch so he wouldn't totally destroy Hammer. And Hawkes still knocked him off his feet with one punch.

That might be one of the last times we see Robert Lufthammer as a Charlestowne Icemen. He leaves the ice, like a boxer who just lost his championship belt trying to quietly make his way out of the ring while the new champ celebrates. Hammer knows his time in Charlestowne is up. The king is dead. Long live the king.

CHAPTER 7

Trade Deadline, Free Fries, and the Flow

Saturday, March 1
Home versus Peninsula win 1–0

Crosby is brilliant again. The Professor makes thirty-two saves, including a spectacular glove save on a breakaway by AHA veteran, Lou Penzeen. Sweet Lou is in all alone and thinks he has Crosby beat clean. But Crosby actually fakes out Penzeen. He gives Lou the glove side high on purpose to shoot at. Penzeen takes the bait, and when he pulls his stick back to shoot, Crosby moves six inches to his left and takes away the glove side. Rubber meets leather with a *thuwump*. After play is stopped, the Professor casually flips the puck out of his glove to the linesman—cool as a witch's tit in a brass bra.

Not too many veteran goalies have the balls to play a breakaway like that, especially against Sweet Lou. Most goalies who leave that glove side exposed are always scared they can't close it quick enough. A twenty-two-year-old rookie pro just made one of the better AHA scorers look like a bender.

Penzeen is shaking his head as he skates past our bench on the way to his own. I chirp at Lou, "Looks like you're the worst player on your team again this season." It's a good-natured jab, and Sweet Lou knows it. He doesn't think I see, but a small smile does cross Penzeen's face.

Monday, March 3
AHA trade deadline

Hammer didn't dress for practice this morning. That's an ominous sign. Trade deadline is today. All moves have to be completed by 3:00 p.m. Eastern time. Since Hammer got smoked in the February 28 practice fight by Hawkes, we all assume Lakor would move or release Lufthammer today. Hammer and Hawkes are essentially the same guy. They certainly have identical hockey skills, and you don't need two goons anymore. One goon will get you into the playoffs, maybe through a round. It doesn't surprise anyone to hear Hammer is on the move.

What surprises *everyone* is *where* Hammer is moving to. It stuns the team. Shock waves roll through the Icemen locker room when we hear Lufthammer is going to division rival, North Jersey! The House Painters needs more grade-A toughness like Lindsay Lohan needs another DUI. You add Hammer to a lineup that already features wild Bill Hunter, that inbred ginger fuck—Aedan Becker—and Seamus O'Malley, suddenly, North Jersey is tougher than the steak special at Waffle House.

In exchange for Hammer, we get Brody Cripenn, a good up-and-down winger, strong defensively. He won't dazzle anyone with his ability to dangle, but offense isn't his game. Cripenn is known for his work ethic and shutdown defensive skills. He's a grinder, a plumber—gritty but with much more talent than Lufthammer. He'll skate on the third line, the checking line, and kill penalties.

This trade makes North Jersey the most physical team in the Eastern division, but it also does a lot for the Icemen. Adding Cripenn to a roster that already features Budler, Karvaala, Slade, and Chrisler gives us the top set of defensive forwards in the division. Every one of our three lines will feature at least one great defensive forward, someone who will cover his man and back-check like his life depends on it. You know what? Come playoff time, every goal is as rare as a hair on Bruce Willis's head. I'd rather be best in the division for defense than cement.

The trade of Lufthammer also means we're going to war with Hawkes as our tough guy, a twenty-year-old heavyweight who has never been tested under AHA playoff pressure. Lakor likes what he sees in One Punch. So do Barnes and I. We have veterans on this team that can play tough: Slade, Hogaboom, Libbet, and myself. We've got Hawkes's six. We know he has ours.

Wednesday, March 5
Home versus Michigan
Win 6–1

This is Chrisler's best game of the season. Keeb gets number 1 star with two goals and leads our PK to five kills in five Michigan chances. *Free small fries* again! Bumpa's Burgers has to be happy with this promotion.

Many of the Section 8 fans are wearing black armbands with a white twenty-eight tonight. That was Hammer's number. This was Bob's sixth season in Charlestowne, and he had become a *real* fan favorite. Some of those die-hards in Section 8 have an eight tattooed over their hearts. I ain't shitting you. I've seen them. If armbands aren't enough mourning, Section 8 did their body painting too. Normal game night features six Section 8ers with body paint spelling out I-C-E-M-E-N. Tonight, those six are spelling out H-A-M-M-E-R.

Even the Icemen employee spinning the game night music salutes Hammer. The first time the body painters and H-A-M-M-E-R hit the ice, he drops the needle on MC Hammer's "Can't Touch This."

Friday, March 7
Home versus Michigan
Win 3–2

Back-to-back home games against the Command. I wish we would schedule some roadies like this for ourselves. When we go all the way out to Elmdale or Springfield, we should play two—saves on travel costs too. Then it dawns on me. There is no travel costs next season. It hits me like getting run over by a city bus. Fuck, the end is getting near.

Sunday, March 9 at Old Market
Lose 6–3

Crosby looks tired all night—a step slow and a split-second off. Barnes needs to sit him soon. Crosby is very quiet after the game. Don't turn inward again on us, Professor.

The oldest player in the AHA, Lancers' goalie, Elmer Hackareinin, beat us again—fourth time this season! You can tell Elmer is old just by that first name. Who the fuck names their boy Elmer anymore? Elmer is so old, he lost his virginity to a Druid. *Retire for fuck's sake!* He's killing us.

Wednesday, March 12

"FUCK! BOOMER! FOR FUCK'S SAKES!" Hogaboom gets a *great* video of this prank for Twitter, both the pre and post prank. When no one is looking, Boomer nails Steele's dress shoes to the bottom of his locker using a nail gun. These are very nice shoes: two-tone black with purple. I'm guessing two hundred dollars for those dandies, imported for sure.

Steele showers after practice, puts on his civilian clothes, and goes to slip on his shoes. They won't budge from the bottom of the locker. Those pneumatic nail guns are the shit. Two nails in each shoe, and Steele might as well replace the locker instead of trying to get those shoes lose. Triple-6 is going nuts. He has to wear his off-ice Nike workout shoes to a lunch date. Hogaboom has Sal video the post-prank explosion by Steele, then email it to him. Boomer is showered and long gone by the time Steele tries to pull on his shoes. The Big Swede is no dummy. He edits the before and after segments together from the safety of home before posting.

Thursday, March 13
Home versus Tech City
Win 7–3

Barnes doesn't like Crosby's last outing against Old Market. He's going to sit the kid over the next two games and play Zeleski. Gutsy move in the heat of a playoff chase, the boys show up for the Z-man, and we win 7–3. Sanderson gets another one from the back line. Hightower and Libbet have two points each. I even get a goal against a pretty good tender, Brad Schultz. *Even a blind hog finds an acorn once in a while*, I think to myself.

Icemen fans at the game get *free small fries again*! We are spoiling them on this last voyage. Libbet is yelling after the game, "Ferda! Ferda boys! Ferda fries!"

Saturday, March 15 at Wilson Falls
Win 2–0

Zeleski goes back-to-back for the first time since November. (*Yes*-vember?) He blocks all twenty-seven Wilson Falls shots in a 2–0 shutout. It is a huge win for Z-man's confidence and our playoff chances.

We can't beat Old Market. But we own these Wilson Falls bitches. We've won all four games against them this season and outscored them 18–4. Who's your daddy, Driftwoods?

We are now within seven points of the fourth and final playoff spot in the East. This is going right down to the final game.

Sunday, March 16

Icemen hockey insider lesson of the month. This month's lesson: keep your poop grouped. That's funny shit.

Second only to sex slang talk, hockey players love to talk shit, literally, and not just talk about their last dump. Several Icemen are known to take pictures with their phones and share the triumph with teammates, especially if the poop is grouped artistically. Slade, Budler,

Chrisler, Lee Harvey, and I all practice this art. I was introduced to this brave new world by Coach Barnes. We were roomies years ago. Barnes proved to me several times that no matter how much shit and toilet paper you crammed in there, it was physically impossible to plug a hotel toilet on floor three or higher simply because of gravity.

Starting at the top, a king coiler is the zenith of shits: perfect color and texture and delicately coiled around the bottom of the bowl to where it overlaps itself, like a coiled-up garden hose. With the right bathroom lighting and cell app, a player can create the Mona Lisa of bowel movements.

As glorious as the king coiler is, there are far more lesser shits that the players talk about and document as art. A king coiler is not the only masterpiece worthy of a digital picture.

Anthill. It has granular texture throughout, wide base, and tapering upward.

Cabbage. Shit that comes out green, typical after beer and eating colored nacho chips.

Camouflage. It is bumpy texture with varying shades of black, brown, and green.

Cantaloupe. A turd that is as wide as it is long. It makes a huge splash. A.K.A. the obese.

Chinese star. It is hard and angular shaped. A.K.A. the Dorito. It hurts upon exiting.

Clean sweep. Shit came out so clean and pristine, there is no poo residue on the first swipe of the toilet paper.

Curtain call. After pulling your pants back up, you feel a rumble. Something drops in your lower GI tract. Round 2 is coming up now.

Dairy queen. It has smooth texture throughout, wide base, tapering upward, and curl at the top.

Déjà poo. Potpourri of colors often contains pieces of vegetables, like corn.

Dunce cap. It has wide base tapering upward to a straight point. If it curls at the top point, you have a dairy queen.

Ghost. It disappears once it hits the toilet. It haunts you, wondering where it went.

Hanging chad. These are stubborn pieces that hang to the anal hair and won't let go. A.K.A. the guard dog.

King coiler. It has perfect color and texture, delicately coiled around the bottom of the bowl to the point where it overlaps itself.

Monster. It has massive girth, extends from the bottom of the bowl upward, and breaks above the waterline. Great relief when it has passed. Second most photographed turd behind the king coiler.

Mudflats. A number 3. It has liquid form, often a violent discharge with very little warning, and leaves streaks in the bowl even after flushing.

Pebble poo. These are small and hard disjointed balls, like rabbit shit.

Peekaboo. A turd that slides into the drain hole, pokes its head out for a second when you flush, then disappears forever down the drain.

Periscope. It has skinny girth. So long it is actually sticking up out of the water.

Rambo. These are traces of blood in your shit or on the toilet paper.

Ring of fire. A burning feeling that grows as the turd slowly works its way out. A.K.A. the flamethrower.

Salad shooter. A form of diarrhea that sprays out of your butt at a rapid pace.

Snake. The long and winding turd, seems like forever to exit your ass.

Soft serve. It is denser than diarrhea but softer than a normal dump. It comes out in one smooth and steady flowing action.

Snake charmer. It is so big that you have to readjust your sitting position on the toilet as it wiggles out. Whistling is optional.

Italian. It is smooth and thin, curls in the bowl like a plate of spaghetti.

Upper decker. You take off the top of the back of the toilet and shit in the reserve tank. That turd is trapped. Every time the toilet is flushed afterward, the bowl fills up with fresh shit water.

Farts have their own language as well. Air biscuit, ass flapper, colon bowling, rectal turbulence, and steam pressing your Calvins are all acceptable hockey slang for a fart.

Monday, March 17

Barnes is really coming into his own this season, going from good coach to great coach. He realizes his team is playing well but tired. We've won nine of our last eleven to make playoff talk legit. No more whispering. After today's morning practice, Barnes gathers the boys around and gives them one and a half days off. "See you Wednesday 11 a.m. for practice." A huge cheer goes up. But before breaking for the day, he leaves them with this Winston Churchill quote: Success is not final; failure is not fatal: it is the courage to continue that counts.

The Backcheck Lounge is overrun by happy, thirsty Icemen. No one quotes Churchill.

Friday, March 21
Home versus Springfield
Win 5–1

Big game for Badinoff. He gets his first hat trick as a pro. Boris scores three completely different goals: slapper from top of the left circle, backhand from right in front, and wrist shot from the left wing, finishing off a three on two break. Badinoff is involved on all five Icemen goals tonight. He assists on the other two goals by Craigsen and LeGault. He's going to have a long career in this game in the NHL.

However, we can't please everybody. Fans are chanting, "We want six. We want fries," for the last seven minutes. They actually booed when the game ends without a sixth goal.

Monday, March 24

Badinoff has his swagger back thanks to Dr. Modato. A couple of veterans get on him about his hair. In the hockey world, hair is sacred. It's revered as much as sex with a rocket or a king coiler dump. Badinoff's hair is every bit as great as his game—long-flowing blond locks, very similar to Fabio or Thor but six inches shorter. Very impressive male-model-quality hair like his is called flow in the hockey world.

Hightower and Bradberry start to razz Boris about his hair. Hightower calls it lettuce. Bradberry asks Boris if he combs it with a piece of toast. It's always so greasy. Badinoff takes it for a bit, let's the veterans chirp, then in his best Russian-tanged broken English, he fires back, "You two! You two! Tell me nah-ding about hair. Nahding. You have none. Zero! Nada! Nul! Zilch. Thero! No hair. Baron [Bradberry], you are fuckt-ing baldt. Baldt motherfucker. Go away." Badinoff says, punctuating his words with a sweeping gesture of his right hand. Then Boris turns his glaze to Hightower. "And you, Leed Harvey. You go away too. You don't have a forehead. You've got a fuckt-ing five head. You are going so baldt." Running his right had now through his flow, Badinoff ends with "Besides, the girls go with the flow." We're all on the flooring literally laughing out loud.

Tuesday, March 25

Bus to Peninsula. DeMarko approaches me as we get close to the hotel and asks me if I'll have dinner with him later tonight. He's up to something. DeMarko never asks me for one-on-one time. He wants something. My Spidey senses are tingling.

I don't want to elevate dinner with DeMarko any higher than it deserves, which is not very high. We have dinner in the empty hotel restaurant. It doesn't take him long to get to his point: This is the last season of the Icemen. He'll need to find a new play-by-play job for next season. He asks me if I'll help and provide him a reference.

As he's prattling on, my mind drifts to his poor wife, Noreen. She must know he's a piece of shit and cheats on her constantly.

Three years ago, he was almost fired by our owner. After an Icemen game, DeMarko pulled some tail out of the Arena Club and brought her back to his office, also in the arena. DeMarko was fucking her doggy style on his desk when the arena cleaning crew opened the door. The cleaners exited as soon as they turned on the lights and saw what was going on. But they did alert arena security. The cleaning crew didn't know DeMarko from Danny DeVito. As far as they know, these could be two fans from Section 8 who broke into the offices. It took security twenty minutes to get to DeMarko's office, but when they did, he was still plowing the puck bunny. Security escorted both out of the arena and filed an incident report. With a paper trail, everyone at the OAMC and Icemen management found out about it. I'm sure the story got back to Noreen at some point.

Listen, I'm no Mormon. But if you want to chase ass like a Kennedy and fuck like Glen Quagmire (giggity), then follow Derek Jeter's example: stay single. Allegedly, that fucker even had a parting gift basket for the girls when they left his apartment the next morning. Also true is that the gift basket included an autographed baseball signed by Derek Jeter. My man! Hall of fame playa! And not just as the Yankees shortstop.

I focus back on DeMarko. He even looks like Quagmire: big head, pointy nose, and wide cheeks. "Sure," I tell him. "I'll keep my ears open." I won't, of course. Fuck him. I wouldn't piss in his mouth if his stomach was on fire.

Wednesday, March 26 at Peninsula
Lose 6–4

We stub our toe in Peninsula, losing by two. Geoff Murcer and Mark Bono skate circles around our D all night. Not a great effort but you can't be a world beater every time out. Just don't slide back into old bad habits. We have to keep grinding and working hard.

I'm eavesdropping on DeMarko as the bus heads back to Charlestowne. Maybe I'm too harsh on him. Should I give him another chance, help him find a job for next season? DeMarko is telling Sal and Chuck about our dinner. Then he shows his true stripes.

After dinner with me, DeMarko sneaks around the corner to a little dive bar. There, he meets the stripper who won our bikini night contest back in mid-January. Her (stage) name is Anastasia. Sweet, thoughtful Anastasia brings runner-up, Tiffany, on the trip as her plus one. DeMarko gets the two strippers drunk and lures them back to his hotel room with promises of coke. The three of them get coked up and then get naked. DeMarko has a threesome with two strippers from Backdoor Jimmy's. No wonder he misses the morning skate. I think maybe it was the clams he had at dinner with me. Turns out it was the clams he had for dessert.

Friday, March 29
Home versus Great Lakes
Win 8–5

What a wild one! We win, and our fans get fatter with free fries. Hightower gets two, one on the old oh-shit move. He's closing in on another forty-goal season. Lee Harvey is going out in style. Libbet and Karvaala have two points each. Crosby isn't great, but when we score 8, he doesn't have to be.

It's that time of the season. Teams in playoff position are battling hard. Teams that are out of it are still trying but at the same time auditioning young guys for next season. Great Lakes has some big six-foot-five goon on their bench. No one has any idea who he is. So new he doesn't even have a nameplate on the back of his jersey. Dude is as dusty as Kathleen Turner's pussy. Poor bastard hasn't hit the ice once all night. All he's done is stand at the end of the Storm bench that is closest to our bench and talk smack.

It's early third period now, and this call-up has *still* not taken one shift. That hasn't stopped him from running his month like he's the second coming of Bob Probert. Hawkes, Slade, Lee Harvey, Hogaboom, Libbet, and me, he's chirped each and every one of us at some point. We're winning 7–2. This kid still hasn't hit the ice, and he's *still* talking shit.

Slade has heard enough. He works his way down to the end of our bench closest to this idiot. Slade moves backup goalie, Zeleski, out of the way so he can get right to the very end of our bench, leans over, and makes sure this asshole hears him. Slade starts to scream, "Who the fuck are you? WHO THE FUCK ARE YOU? Turn around so I can see the name on the back of your jersey. No name. Then start walking. Go back to the fucking beer league you came out of." The Storm call-up tries to rally with some fresh material. But he is done after that. And he never does hit the ice. He shows up as a DNP (dressed, did not play) on the game summary sheet.

Steele, Hogaboom, and Crosby all post Slade's rant on their twitter. It is that classic.

CHAPTER 8

Nosey Guys, Yoda, and Beatdowns

Tuesday, April 1
Home versus Tri-Cities
Win 2–1

Boomer can't help himself on April Fools' Day. He convinces Steele to join him on a prank at our game tonight. They both tweet out beforehand that it's free-money night with the Icemen. Several of the Olympia Arena ushers have crisp, new one-hundred-dollar bills on them. You just need to figure out which ones! Walk up to any usher at tonight's game and ask them, "Are you a hundred?" If the answer is yes, you've just won one hundred dollars.

No such promotion exists. The ushers ain't exactly following Boomer and Triple-6 on Twitter. They don't have a clue why all these fans are coming up to them and asking, "Are you a hundred?" Some of the ushers are close to one hundred years old. They are almost all retirees doing this for walking-around money. They are not amused.

We're really playing playoff-style hockey at the moment. Tonight's win puts the Icemen only six points out of the fourth and final playoff spot in the East with nine games left to play. We can do this! Crosby does his part tonight, notched his eighteenth win of the season. The Professor will get at least twenty in his first year as a pro. I'm not sure whose NHL future is brighter at the moment: Badinoff or Crosby. They'll both be all-stars in the show in two to three years. We might have two remember whens on this final Icemen team.

While on the topic of rising stars. Jon Sanderson. It's been two and a half months already since we picked him up on waivers from Highland. We are lucky to get Machine. Sanderson is fuckin' money.

Waiver claim is based on the team records *in reverse order*. When someone goes on waivers, the first option to claim him goes to the team with the worst record in the league. Our record was so bad when the Kilt Lifters waived Sanderson, we were sixth in line. Five AHA teams with worse records than us on January 15 passed on Jon. They all had their own reasons: not in the playoff chase, didn't want to add expense, and already deep on defense. Machine fell to us at number 6, and Lakor jumped on him.

He fits right in with the culture here. Tonight, Sandy gets under the skin of Thunderbirds superstar, Brock Hayes, and takes him right out of the game. Hayes wears a full visor and likes to run his mouth. He's also been known to beat his girlfriend. Hayes is attempting to irritate Sanderson with a Tourette's syndrome explosion of cuss words wrapped in a surfer bum slur. Sandy makes a cranking motion with his right hand and says to Hayes, "Hey, Bro J Simpson. Roll down your window. I can't hear you through the glass." Hayes spends the rest of the night trying to catch Sandy and forgets about doing what he's paid to do: score goals.

The more I'm around Sanderson, the more I think he has a little Rickey Henderson in him. Machine has trouble remembering names. When he first got here, I chalked it up to coming to a new team in a new division. Machine didn't see a lot of us playing for Highland in the Western Division the last several years. In the off-season, he's surfing, not golfing, so he wouldn't bump into our Canadian guys on the course. This would explain Jon's excessive use of bro terminology when talking to his teammates: He doesn't know our fucking names!

Baseball hall of famer, Rickey Henderson, could *not* remember his teammates' names. He used to refer to them by the position they played. "Great throw, catcher," or "Get a hit now, third baseman."

Henderson signed with Seattle in 2000. In Mariners spring training that year, Rickey was shagging balls, standing next to the team's veteran first baseman, Jon Olerud. Olerud wore a batting helmet while in the field on defense.

Rickey said, "Hey, first baseman. Why do you always wear a batting helmet while playing first?"

Olerud said, "To protect my head. I had an aneurysm years ago in college."

Rickey said, "Man, I played with someone like that with the Blue Jays. He wore a helmet in the field too."

Olerud said, "Yeah, Rickey. That was me. We played together in Toronto for two seasons."

Sanderson may not know their first names, but it's no coincidence both Icemen goalies have improved since he got here. He is huge tonight: assist on the GWG and blocking six shots.

Thursday, April 3
Home versus Musktown
Win 5–3

This is a pretty uneventful game until the end. Then it escalates quickly to ugly.

Game is almost over, less than a minute to play. We're winning 5–3. The Generals are frustrated. They think they're a better team than us. They feel they should have won this game. Our third line, the checking line, is on the ice for the final minute. Musktown coach, Rupert Blumpkin, has his top-scoring line out there, trying to pull off a miracle. Blumpkin sees Hawkes out there. He decides to send a message instead of trying to score two late goals and force OT. Over the Generals' boards comes their goon, Matt Wilsen. It's obvious why a stonehand cement head like Wilsen is out there with less than a minute to go and down by two goals. And it's not for his scoring prowess.

Play goes into our end. Crosby makes a couple of easy saves, falls to his knees, and covers the puck. Wilsen doesn't care the puck is frozen or that the ref blows his whistle. Wilsen crashes into Crosby and sends him sprawling. Steele grabs Wilsen. They wrestle for a couple of seconds before players from both teams race in—more pushing and shoving and face washes. Now it's a scrum of seven players in front of Crosby. They all collapse on each other into a pile. Wilsen and Steele are at the bottom of that pile. Steele is on his back on the ice. Wilsen is on top of him. They're nose to nose. Their arms are pinned by the crush of other players on top of them.

They can't do much but trash-talk. Wilsen is still jawing at Steele, calling him names like Triple-6 devil fuck and crazy motherfucker. Steele responds with a line from the great film *Chinatown*, "Do you know what happens to nosey people?" Before Wilsen can answer, Steele channels his inner Mike Tyson. Steele suddenly lunges forward with only his head and bites off the tip of Wilsen's nose.

Wilsen is screaming now, making scared, panic-like noises you never hear in a hockey fight—noises you would make if locked in a phone booth with a hungry Dr. Hannibal Lecter. Players from both teams realize something isn't right. They get up off Wilsen and Steele. Granted freedom, Wilsen is up and away from Steele. He bolts down the Generals' tunnel. There is blood everywhere at the bottom of the pile. No one yet realizes what the fuck happened. Steele skates back to our bench like he's strolling through the Palace of Versailles gardens. The refs figure it out shortly thereafter. Steele gets a game and a gross misconduct. Suspension was sure to follow. While in the locker room, he tweets about the whole thing, "If you're going to be crazy, you have to get paid for it or else you're going to be locked up."

My man. Hunter S. Thompson. Fear and loathing with the Icemen.

Saturday, April 5
Home versus Wilson Falls
Win 5–2

You want the good news first or the bad news? Okay, the good news. Our dominance over Wilson Falls continues. Tonight's 5–2 victory makes us 5–0 so far this season against these losers. Ten points out of possible ten points. Perfecto!

NOSEY GUYS, YODA, AND BEATDOWNS

other stooge like Mac Becholay or Leo Hibbert. Maybe all three of those fuckers.

The history between Bootman and me. He's a year younger. He's a Detroit kid too, East Sider. Or Eastpointe as it's now called. White Boy Rick and other drug dealers destroyed the quality of life in Detroit back in late 1980s / early 1990s. People on that side of Detroit thought if they changed the name from East Detroit to Eastpointe, it would change people's perceptions. Dumb East Side fucks. Like putting pointe in the name is going to make people think you are more Grosse Pointe than you are Detroit. That's literally putting lipstick on a pig.

Fifteen years ago, I almost killed Bootman on an icing call. Right off the opening face-off, the puck was shot into our end. I was starting on D, so I turned and chased. Bootman was right behind, racing me for the puck. He was jabbing at the back of my legs, on the calf where there was no padding. I was getting pissed. I know who it was. As we got near the end boards, I stopped skating forward and turned around to face Bootman. I was skating backward now. I grabbed him. Two strides from the end glass, I spun back around, still holding Bootman. With him in front now, I ran Bootman ass first into the end boards as hard as I can. I accentuated the violence with my right forearm across this throat, driving his head into the glass. Bootman went down in a heap and did not move. They took him out on a stretcher. He was still not moving. I was beginning to worry now that I killed Bootman or at least fucked him up badly. He was okay. CAT scan. Overnight hospital stay. Concussion. But he'll live to fight another day.

And fight we have. Since we both turned pro, I've fought Bootman maybe twenty times—another half dozen or so fights in amateur. When it comes to my record versus Bootman, I haven't won them all. But I have showed up for every one of them. And I'll show up again Sunday night in Wilson Falls.

The bad news. This is a home-and-home series. Our last game against the Driftwoods is tomorrow night in their barn. And I had to go and break The Code tonight.

Steele is suspended, of course, for making an appetizer out of Matt Wilsen's nose. Slade is dinged up, didn't dress. Hawkes does play but limited. He's hurting too. Driftwoods tough guy, Bill Bootman, is taking advantage of our dearth of toughness. He is running my team-mates all over the rink all night long. I feel it is my job to settle this asshole Bootman down. My feelings on this topic are compounded by the fact Bootman and I have a long history playing against each other, dating back to fourteen-year-olds in bantam hockey.

Bootman lines up Chrisler in front of our bench. There's no glass in front of the bench, of course, so players can jump on and off and change on the fly. He runs him hard into the glass and stanchion at the far end of our bench where the glass starts up again to protect the fans. The glass forms a right angle in that spot. It's a very danger-ous area. Most players would pull up a bit from their check in this location, especially on a little guy like Chrisler. Not Bootman. He makes sure he gets Chrisler all wrapped up before plowing him into that intersection of stanchion and glass.

I snap. I yell at Bootman. He turns, looks at me, nods his head in that asking manner, and says, "You wanna go?" I nod yes. Chrisler crawls to our bench. I take his spot on the ice and go right up to Bootman. Play is at the other end of the rink by now. Bootman and I drop our sticks and gloves, still in front of the Icemen bench. We're alone. We dance around a bit, jockeying to land that first punch. Suddenly, Bootman is falling to the ice. He steps on one of his own gloves. Down he goes! I can't help myself. While Bootman is defense-less and on his back, I jump on top of him. Two quick rights to the snot locker while he's lying there. The linesmen pull me off.

I broke The Code rule number 5. I know it. Bootman knows it. Tomorrow night in Wilson Falls, I'll be a man and live up to The Code rule number 7: Everybody gets a rematch.

After the game, we take the bus to Wilson Falls. I can't sleep. I know I owe Bootman that rematch. I'll have to fight him or some

Sunday, April 6 at Wilson Falls
Lose 6–5 in overtime

Right from warm-ups, the Driftwoods start chirping me about breaking The Code last night. Bootman, Becholay, and Mark Tudano are all running their mouths. Hell, even their goalie, Todd Van Randle, is giving me shit. And he's a fucking goalie! That's like an NFL punter threatening to body slam a defensive end. I am getting more than lip service from the Driftwoods. Three times during warm-ups, a puck from the Wilson Falls' end is fired into our end and hit me hard on the side of my foot—not an accident, not three times! Even with skates on, that stings a bit. I know what I'm in for. That's why I couldn't sleep on the bus ride last night or take a pre-game nap today.

I tell my teammates after warm-up that I *have* to get this rematch over with. The first time Bootman is on the ice, change up your line immediately, so I can get out there and take care of business. Once Bootman gets his rematch, I can worry about playing hockey.

It doesn't take long. Bootman jumps over the boards for the second shift of the first period with 16:20 left to play. Karvaala gets it. Once he sees Bootman hit the ice, Karvaala slams on the brakes and makes a beeline to our bench. Over I go to replace him at right wing.

Bootman sees me as I come into our defensive zone. He knows. I know. The Icemen know. The Driftwoods know. The referees and linesmen know. The 7,428 fans on hand tonight in Wilson Falls know. Here comes the rematch. A quote from my man, Hunter S. Thompson, flashes across my mind as I line-up Bootman: *Buy the ticket, take the ride.*

Bradberry semi-purposely slides the puck over to his own goalie, and Zeleski freezes it. A whistle and play is stopped. The other ten players are clustered close to the Icemen net. Bootman and I have maneuvered ourselves into open ice between the two face-off circles and only a couple of feet inside the blue line. We remove our gloves and helmets, setting them down gently on the ice, not just tossing them down. We tug up on our elbow pads and make sure they have not slipped down and could encumber our ability to throw a punch.

Bootman and I square up. We've done this dance many times before. We know each other's moves and preferences. Not a word is said between us. The crowd is on their feet and yelling as loud as they can.

Most hockey fights are spontaneous. You really don't have time to think about it. You just react. Drop the gloves and start to trade hands. This one is different. Both Bootman and I know we are going to fight tonight. We've had twenty-four hours to think about strategy or overthink strategy, which is my first mistake.

I'm no heavyweight like Hawkes. My right hand is decent, but the other guy doesn't go to DEFCON 1 when he fights me. Bootman knows this. He knows more about what I can do to him with my right hand than what his wife can do to him with hers. I've been thinking about this one moment for twenty-four hours now.

I decide to go off script and try to win this thing with one big knockout punch. I fake the left jab (which I *always* open with) and throw a haymaker of a right hand. This punch has got serious steam behind it. I've caught Bootman off balance. He bites on the fake left jab. But this isn't his first rodeo either. Bootman sees my right streaking for his chin and ducks at the last second. I hit him hard but on the top of the head. If that punch had landed on his chin, it would have been nighty night.

Bootman now knows I'm not going by the book. I put everything I have into loading up that right hand and winning the fight on one big thunderbolt. When I threw the right, the follow through forced me to drop my left hand. Now I'm the guy off balance with an open left side. Bootman takes advantage and pops me with two quick right jabs. The second one catches my nose and draws a trickle of blood. We lock up by grabbing a handful of each other's jerseys with our left hands and start to fire right hands at each other in quick, machine-gun-like flurries: jabs, hooks, straights, and uppercuts. As soon as one right lands, the other guy retaliates with his own right.

We stand toe-to-toe and slam away. No one is playing defense at all. The crowd gets louder and louder with every punch. This exchange goes on for a good forty-five seconds. We are both worn out. Bootman lands a straight right that hits me on the button. That's it. I'm done. I'm exhausted, dazed, and falling to the ice. Bootman is out of gas too. As I fall, he still has a left hand full of my jersey. Bootman doesn't have the energy to let go. I drag him down with me. We hit the ice. The linesmen jump in. The crowd gives us a standing ovation. Players on both benches are banging their sticks on the boards, a hockey salute to their respective teammate. As you head to the penalty box, your teammates are lightly tapping your shin guards with their sticks. You can tell by the look in your teammate's eyes they just witnessed something special.

Sitting in the penalty box with an ice bag on my right hand, I glance to my left. Bootman is already looking at me from his penalty box. Neither one of us blinks. Bootman then cocks his head, rolls his eyes in a circle, and mouths, "Wow." I smile and wink back at him—rematch granted, The Code reinstated. We play hockey for the rest of the game.

Afterward, DeMarko gives me the punch count. He watched the replay of the fight during the first intermission on the Wilson Falls' coaches' video. DeMarko scores it eighteen punches landed by Bootman and seventeen punches by me. One knockdown. Bootman wins on a split decision. Okay. I'll accept the judge's scorecards. But I did show up.

Oh, we lose the game in overtime 6–5. That keeps us from sweeping the season series against these assholes Final season record in six head-to-head games: 5-0-1. Eleven of a possible twelve points—not too shabby. If we do make the playoffs, a lot of credit will go to us kicking the shit out of Wilson Falls all season.

Thursday, April 10
Home versus Gotham
Win 5–0

After the morning skates, I run into an old friend, Metros forward, Erik Luhtanen. He tells me a great Coach Haynesworth story from their last road trip.

Gotham's bus pulled up to the hotel, and Haynsie was off like he was launched from an artillery cannon. He didn't grab his bags and didn't check in and grab his room key. Haynesworth literally ran into the hotel lobby and straight to the men's room.

A few minutes later, he came out of the lobby bathroom. A handful of the players, including Luhtanen, were still checking into the hotel. As Haynesworth walked by, the players shot him curious but respectable glances. They were just a bit concerned with their sixty-five-year-old coach's urgency. As he reached the group, Haynsie paused to say, "Boys, one day, you'll be my age. When you are, remember these three things: Never pass up a bathroom. Never trust a fart. Honor every hard on."

And with those words of wisdom, Haynesworth had his room key, was around the corner, and headed to the hotel elevator bank.

Crosby with another shutout and his twentieth win of the season. He's playoff ready right now. Cripenn breaks out with two goals. That's huge. We get Brody because of his great defense. Anything he scores is a bonus.

I shake hands with Haynesworth immediately after the game. "See ya on the nineteenth," he says. "That one could be winner take all for the final playoff spot." Easy, Yoda. Don't play your Jedi mind tricks on me. Haynsie wants me to think we'll still be in a playoff race in nine more days. We've got two huge division games to worry about first.

Saturday, April 12

"FUCK! BOOMER! FOR FUCK'S SAKES!" Lee Harvey is on the ice, shaking his head and holding half a hockey stick. Hogaboom saws the blade nearly all the way through, then covers it with hockey tape. The evil genius that he is, Boomer retapes the stick with old used tape. If Hightower had seen new fresh white tape on his practice twig, he'd have clued in right away.

He doesn't. Hightower steps on the ice for practice, taking his first warm-up lap. He scoops up a puck and lazily slides it toward the net. He doesn't shoot the puck, slides it. The blade immediately snaps in two, held together only by the hockey tape. *Boomer!* Hogaboom, on the ice as well for practice, ignores Lee Harvey. Chuck, the equipment guy, frowns and curses. This shit is hitting close to home for him, impacting his potential budget bonus!

Sunday, April 13
Home versus North Jersey
Win 5–4

Slade wins it with a late goal. Evil Roy tucks a rebound underneath Bobby Ennet (not to be confused with his goaltender brother, Billy Ennet) from the doorstep. It reminds me of a Section 8 T-shirt from a few seasons ago: Jesus saves, but Slade scores on the rebound.

It is a monstrous win for us against a very good team. Icemen are now just two points away from clinching the fourth and final play spot in the Eastern division. If we can beat Old Market on Wednesday *or* Gotham Saturday, we clinch fourth in the East. And that, my friends, gets your playoff ticket punched.

This game has a definite playoff feel to it. There is plenty of kaboom going on. Hogaboom was sending messages to the House Painters: Better keep your head up or I'll fucking steamroll you.

After every big Boomer hit, there is a scrum on the whistle—lots of face washes, the other team punching you in the nuts, and a couple of pretty good scraps too. In his first game back from Nose Gate, Steele pounds Seamus O'Malley. That is payback for the January 28 game when O'Malley gave Chrisler an Irish handshake, a nasty headbutt. Slade fills in Wild Bill Hunter. One ominous sign though: Hammer does not dress. He doesn't even come by the morning skate to say hello to his old teammates. I'll translate that into he's pissed at the Icemen and can't wait for a chance to get his.

I'll bet after this one, both teams are loaded down with ice bags on their sore spots. I know we are.

If we do sneak into the playoffs, we'll draw these fuckers in round 1. They'll be first in the division. We'll be fourth. If that happens, both teams better buckle their chin straps and pack a lunch. It's gonna be a *long* trip.

Wednesday, April 16
Home versus Old Market
Lose 3–0

A great opportunity for the Icemen tonight, and we blow it. We could have clinched a playoff spot with a win in front of the home fans. Section 8 is primed for it. But we shit the bed and lose 3–0 as fucking Hackareinin shuts us out again! WTF. This guy is so old, his first STD was the bubonic plague. Old Market owns us. In six games against them this season, we won only one.

There was an omen before the game that this wasn't going to be our night. The Icemen marketing department, in recognition of our thirty-eighth and final season in the AHA, did a nice giveaway item for the fans attending tonight's game: a commemorative throw blanket featuring the Icemen logo and the four times we've won the AHA Koontz Cup championship.

Four times in thirty-seven years with this season TBD. Great blanket, except two of the four seasons noted on the blanket are wrong. Fuck. Doesn't anyone proof this shit before it goes into production? I'm told this is a pet project of B R-squared, the owner's son. He ran with it the whole way. Silver lining on this B R-squared project: No one fell out of a helicopter and died while hunting wild hogs with .50 calibers.

What a shame to lose this game. Our fans are ready to party! Instead, after a crushing loss, the Arena Lounge is like a morgue. Our fans think we could blow this and not make the playoffs. Could we actually lose the last three regular season games when all we have to do is win one to make the playoffs?

In our last season of existence, who knows what the hockey gods have in store for us? Gotta go to Gotham now Saturday and beat Yoda to get into the playoffs. Do or do not. There is no try.

Saturday, April 19 at Gotham
Win 7–3

Don't let that final score deceive you. It is a much closer game than that, much closer. We are tied 2–2 after two periods. Gotham scores a sloppy goal in the first minute of third period to go up 3–2. I can see the boys squeezing their sticks. We are choking worse than a Charlie Sheen hooker. If we lose this one, it's a *must-win* Sunday at home versus an Elmdale team that has nothing to play for, except to fuck up our final season. No one wants that scenario.

Still losing 3–2 at the fifteen-minute mark of the third, Badinoff makes an unbelievable deke to go around defenseman Stephan Ryan and ties game at 3–3. Two minutes later, we get a power play when Metros' Pete Hickey takes a stupid slashing call away from the play. Cripenn steps into a one-timer from the point for a PPG, and suddenly, we lead 4–3. With eight minutes to play, Lee Harvey strikes. Number 22 gets number 42 on the year, and just like that, we have all the Mo, leading 5–3. Haynesworth pulls his goalie, Karl Ruttan, with three minutes to go. They need a win, too, to stay in the playoff hunt. Two empty net goals later, we win 7–3. The Icemen are going to the AHA playoffs!

Haynesworth, like Yoda, is always right. Ten days ago, after losing to us 5–0, Haynesworth told Barnes and I that this game tonight "could be a winner take all for the fourth playoff spot." He was dead on. The Icemen make me proud tonight. This is our first win all season in Gotham, and it couldn't have come at a more opportune time.

Haynesworth is such a classy person. His team has just been eliminated from playoff contention. After speaking with his team, Haynesworth comes over to our dressing room. He congratulates our entire team and makes special note of the opportunity in front of us, "Your organization's last season, last playoff run. Make it memorable for the fans but also for you. For some of you, that last playoff game will be your last as a pro hockey player.

"Many of you will keep on playing here in the AHA or the NHL. But you may never have a playoff experience again like the one you *could* have starting next week. I'm rooting for you to make history as you close out history of the Icemen in Charlestowne."

I'm a little misty eyed after that one, so are Libbet and Hightower. This is likely the end of the road for them. Maybe me too.

Lots of beer and fun on the bus ride back home. The pressure is off now for the regular season finale back in Charlestowne. We've clinched the fourth spot and locks us into a first-round matchup with North Jersey, the number 1 seed in the East. Lots of Icemen fans had traveled to the game in Gotham and watched us clinch. There is quite a caravan of vehicles going south back to Charlestowne. Everyone is relieved we don't have to win tomorrow at home against Elmdale to make the playoffs.

Sunday, April 20
Home versus Elmdale
Lose 6–1

It was the best of times. It was the worst of times. Tonight is the last regular season home game in the thirty-eight-year history of the Icemen. The Koontz Cup playoffs start next week.

We are pretty lifeless and lose a meaningless game 6–1. No one cares except to *not* get hurt. Win or lose, we open at North Jersey next week.

We rest a few of the vets tonight. I don't dress. Budler is still playing for keeps, like he's fighting for the last loaf in a Czech breadline. Second intermission in the locker room, Buzz asks me to check on something for him.

Budler says, "Can you check the AHA record book for most players, one team one season, with over one hundred penalty minutes?"

I say, "What the fuck? Why do you need to know that?"

Budler says, "DeMarko tells me we've tied the all-time AHA record for most players, one team one season, with over one hundred penalty minutes. The record is nine, and we have nine guys with one hundred or more minutes."

I say, "And this is important because?"

Budler says, "I've got ninety-two minutes! If I can get a misconduct in the third period, I'll have 102 minutes and be our tenth guy over one hundred. That will give us the all-time AHA record!"

I say, "Conversation over. I want NO part of this."

Four minutes are left in the third period. We are down 5–1 and have nothing to play for. Budler is out there to take a face-off against the Elmos' top line center, Barry Stefford. Budler won't get in position for the face-off. He's arguing with the linesmen in a very animated way. After a loud and lengthy discussion, the referee comes over to see what the issue is. Budler turns his scorn to the referee. Nose to nose, they are both agitated and waving their arms around.

The crowd is growing restless over the delay. They start to boo loudly. "Drop the puck!" A couple of items are thrown on the ice. The referee stares at Budler. Finally, the ref bounces a hand off each hip in that quick downward motion—a ten-minute misconduct for Budler. He's done for the day. And he's got his 102 penalty minutes.

I go up to the Red Baron postgame. "Okay, now I have to hear the story. What the fuck did you say to the referee to get a ten-minute misconduct?" Budler draws in a deep breath.

"I went through the same thing with him that I went through with the linesman and with you: AHA record for most players, one team one season, with over one hundred penalty minutes is nine. We've tied the record. I've got ninety-two minutes. Give me ten, and we have ten guys over one hundred minutes—new record. Linesman says to me, 'Blah, blah, blah. Line up, or I'll drop the puck without you.' I step up my argument, getting louder. The referee comes over. I give him the same rant: AHA record. We've tied it with nine. I need a misconduct to set the new record. Ref is not moved. He's screaming at me to play hockey. I lean in close to the ref and say, 'Listen to that crowd. We can do this the easy way or the hard way. You can give me ten minutes right now. Or I'll go over there"—nodding toward our bench—"empty out the stick rack, and you'll have a fuckin' riot on your hands. Ref looks at me, thinks for a minute, and then BAM. He says, 'There's your ten minutes. Congratulations on the new record. Now get the fuck off my ice.'"

And that's how the Icemen closed out the last regular season game in their thirty-eight-year history. If you want to know wins and losses, our final regular season record is 37-32-5.

What a roller-coaster ride it is. Our record through December was 14-19-3. That was a minor miracle itself. Icemen won as many games in the month of December, seven, as we did October and November combined. Starting in January, we went 23-13-2, winning nine our last fourteen games. We also beat Gotham twice and North Jersey once in a nine-day stretch in April. That's coming up big when it counted.

Peaking at the right moment? We'll find out soon, in three days, against the best team in the history of the league.

CHAPTER 9

Playoffs! Playoffs?

Monday, April 21

Put the shovels down. We're not dead yet. One last AHA playoff appearance for the Icemen before we're put on waivers forever and claimed by the dustbin of hockey history.

This crazy last season started back on October 12. We entertained a sellout home crowd with a 6–1 ass beating of Wilson Falls (that would become a habit of ours over the season). That night also featured the first of seven *free french fries* nights during the season. If the Icemen score six or more goals, then fans can redeem their ticket stubs at any Bumpa's Burgers for a free small fry. I hope Icemen fans enjoyed it during the regular season. Playoffs are a whole different animal: tighter checking, more aggressive defense, referees lose their whistles for long stretches, and less shots on goal and scoring chances. Six goals in the playoffs could very likely be what you get for two post season games.

I won't say this out loud. Even if we get swept in the first round, we're already winners. It's a victory just to make the playoffs. Our fans are delirious about making the postseason, "Just happy to be here." After thirty-seven years in Charlestowne, this thirty-eighth season is the finale. Finis. The end. Closed permanently. Forever. Ceased. Death. We knew that going into the season and could have easily spit out the bit and given up. Instead, we battled back from a horrendous first two months and snuck into the fourth spot in the American Hockey Association Eastern Division on the second-to-last game of the regular season. Our reward? In round 1, we'll face our archrival, North Jersey. The House Painters are coming off a year in which they smashed the previous AHA records for most regular season wins, most regular season points, and most goals scored one team one season.

How did we end up facing North Jersey? There are sixteen teams in the AHA, and the top four teams in the Eastern and Western Divisions make the Koontz Cup playoffs. In the first round (aka as the Eastern Division semifinals), the number 1 team in the East (North Jersey) opens at home against the number 4 team in the East (your Icemen). When you look at our regular season effort against them, we did okay: played six times, won two, lost three, and lost the other game in overtime. The good news: At home, we won two of the three games, losing that third home game in overtime. The bad news: At North Jersey, we lost all three games. Goals scored in the six games are misleading too. Overall, North Jersey outscored us 25–20. But in the three games in their barn, we were outscored 16–9. This postseason series is best of seven. First team to win four advances. We have only three home games. So somewhere in the series, we'll need to win a game in North Jersey.

There is genuine hatred between these two teams. We detest each other. I hate North Jersey more than Pavarotti hates a scale. This is a rivalry just short of USA versus ISIS. Playoff hockey by nature is much more of a physical grind than the regular season. Add in a playoff opponent you despise, and the physicality just gets amped up a couple of more notches.

Fuel for the fire.

We just set the AHA single season record for most players on one team with over one hundred penalty minutes. But North Jersey has three legitimate heavyweights, and we have just one, rookie Todd Hawkes.

One of the House Painters' heavyweights was a beloved Icemen teammate for six seasons. On March 3, Robert Lufthammer was traded to North Jersey for Brody Cripenn. Hammer is the real deal. So are the House Painters' Aedan Becker and Wild Bill Hunter. I wouldn't put Seamus O'Malley in their heavyweight class, but he's a handful for anyone that wants to tangle with him. O'Malley is as likely to hit you with an Irish handshake (headbutt) as he is with a fist.

Finally, there's the little matter of that bench-clearing brawl on December 11 in their barn. It started on the ice between the two teams, then spilled into the stands behind our bench. Icemen players, coaches, and trainers ended up fighting the House Painters' fans.

I'm sure we'll get a warm welcome from the North Jersey fans for game 1. All this playoff matchup is missing is Michael Buffer live to declare "LET'S get ready to RUMBLE!"

Koontz Cup playoffs
AHA Eastern Division Semifinals Game 1
Wednesday, April 23 at North Jersey
Lose 3–2

It is a very strange way to start the playoffs. None of us had even contemplated this. Less than a minute into the pregame warm-up, North Jersey fans start chanting "Hammer. Hammer. Hammer."

After six years of serenading from Icemen fans, it is surreal to hear that in an opponent's arena.

A couple of us sneak a glance at the House Painters' end of the ice, looking for Lufthammer. There he is, wearing his number 28 jersey and staring back at us. Hammer has not spoken to one player on our team since the trade. He's going to want to make a point early in game 1.

We're all a bit unnerved and intimidated in the first period. Crosby gives up a goal to Bob Barbour on the first shot on the game, less than one-minute in. The crowd goes absolutely apeshit, but the Professor doesn't panic. He settles down after that and plays well. The defense in front of him is a mixed bag. The younger D struggle in their first playoff game as pros (Steele and Richatelli). But the veteran D (LeGault, Sanderson, Hogaboom, and Bradberry) balance them out.

A third period power play goal by Gerry Coleman is the difference. Craigsen is in the box on a debatable interference call.

Hammer does get his wish in the first period. He gets to drop the mitts with Hawkes. Each heavy lands a couple of shots but no knockdowns or knockouts. Call it a draw.

Steele, on the other hand, crushes that ginger fuckface, Becker, later in the game. Becker, at first, didn't want to go with Steele, then did so reluctantly. The legend of Steele's dead dog in the freezer and biting off an opponent's nose can have that effect.

Koontz Cup playoffs
AHA Eastern Division Semifinals Game 2
Friday, April 25 at North Jersey
Win 5–2; series tied 1–1

We surprise the House Painters tonight. They are overconfident after game 1, our fourth straight loss in their arena this season. Scoring another early goal on Crosby helps put air in their tires. Professor stops thirty of thirty-one shots after that.

A PPG goal from Lee Harvey on a beautiful one-timer ties it up. Slade gets a power play goal early in the second to put us ahead to stay. Machine has two assists including one on Libbet's empty net goal to make the final 5–2.

We take the game we need in their arena. We are headed back home now, tied 1–1. We now have the home ice advantage. It's a happy but subdued ride to Charlestowne. We've only won one game, albeit a huge one. We still have a long way to go to get four wins against the best team in the history of the AHA.

Sunday, April 27

LeGault's smoke booth is completely disassembled, laying on the arena floor in pieces.

OAMC claims there is a ventilation problem. I'm not sure how anyone would know that. No one smokes in there except LeGault. Come on, man, this is the playoffs! Fix the man's smoke booth!

Koontz Cup playoffs
AHA Eastern Division Semifinals Game 3
Monday, April 28
Home versus North Jersey; win 2–0

Charlestowne leads series two games to one, Crosby steals one, and there are 9,819 witnesses to his robbery. This is the Icemen's first home playoff game in eight years, and we are badly exposed. Crosby stops thirty-eight shots, including several spectacular, SportsCenter-quality saves.

Budler has a hand in both our goals, scoring what turned out to be the game winner in the second period and assisting on Badinoff's in the third. Dale spends the night doing his thing: disturbing shit, irritating the House Painters' top line, and taking them off their game. Budler buzzes around all night and is named the number 2 star of the game after the Professor.

We've won the pivotal game 3. AHA history will tell you when a best of seven is tied at one game each, the winner of game 3 goes on to win the series 69 percent of the time. I like history. I hope history likes the Icemen on this one.

Koontz Cup playoffs
AHA Eastern Division Semifinals Game 4
Wednesday, April 30
Home versus North Jersey
Lose 4–2; series tied 2–2

Fuck me. As soon as we get in the driver's seat, we go over a cliff. With a win tonight, the Icemen could have been in complete control of this series, up three games to one. Instead, we lose game 4, at home, 4–2. Rather than being up 3–1, the series is now tied 2–2. It's a best of three from here on out, and the House Painters have two of those three in their home arena. We'll now have to go in there and win *another* one to win the playoff series.

It was a hard-fought game but then close only counts in horse-shoes, curling, and field artillery.

Hammer hammers Steele in a lopsided fight. House Painters' goalie, Bob Ennet (not to be confused with brother goalie, Bill), takes over after that. He is tighter than the fourteen-year-old female hosts at a Jeffrey Epstein sleepover.

Very, very gloomy in the Arena Lounge after the game. It has the feel and smell of dead dreams. I stop in for one quick vodka/tonic before going home. "It was a good run" is the general consensus from our fans. "Didn't think we'd make the playoffs, and we did. What more can you ask for in the team's final season? There is no way we can win a *second* game this playoff round at North Jersey. Game 6 back here in Charlestowne on Sunday is likely the last game ever in the history of the Icemen." I'm glad a fearless twenty-year-old rookie from frozen Nunavut isn't paying attention.

Koontz Cup playoffs
AHA Eastern Division Semifinals Game 5
Friday, May 2 at North Jersey
Win 6–4; Charlestowne leads series three games to two

We are tied 3–3 in game 5 but really holding on for our playoff lives. The House Painters *want* this one. Any advantage we had from being disrespected and under estimated is over.

They are buzzing our net, outhitting us, and taking away our scoring chances. We're on the ropes, and the best team in AHA history is looking for the kill shot.

And then game 5 turns around in the wink of an eye, more like the flash of a right fist.

Game 5 is still tied 3–3, 3:45 left in the second period. We're lining up for a face-off right in front of the North Jersey bench. Hawkes is out there as part of Budler's line. While guys are getting set, Hawkes looks at North Jersey coach, Bobby O'Rablow, and yells,

"Hey, ya little fat fuck. Why don't you tell your boys to take their skirts off?"

Now I don't need to tell you how big of balls are required to make that comment to that coach in that arena at that point in the game. Hawkes is either the most confident twenty-year-old fighter I have ever played with or has a death wish. Coach O'Rablow has smoke coming out of his ears. He pulls Wild Bill Hunter off the ice and sends out Hammer to deal with Hawkes.

Everyone knows it's *go time* right off the face-off. In fact, the two centers taking the draw don't even make an effort when the linesman drops the puck. They stand straight up to watch.

Hawkes and Hammer skate directly to center ice. They size each other up, then move closer.

Other players move away so the two heavies have all the room they need. Players settle into their ringside seats. The fans are on their feet screaming, "Hammer. Hammer. Hammer." Hawkes decides to engage right away and not sit back, which is what the book is on his style. Hawkes makes another change. His first punch is a right hand cross instead of the overhand bomb.

Hammer is looking for the bomb, not expecting the right cross, and it catches him right on the jaw. Hammer is stunned by the first punch. His knees buckle. As he's falling to the ice, Hawkes *then* throws the bomb. *Boom!* Straight right hand hits Hammer flush in the face and drives him down onto the ice. The building goes silent. You could hear a beer drop. Hammer is out cold at center ice, blood dripping from his nose and mouth. Hawkes skates away making the belt motion across his waist. Unanimous decision: The heavyweight championship stays with the kid from Nunavut.

On the very next shift, Craigsen scores on a terrific cross goalmouth pass from Karvaala, and we take a 4–3 lead into the locker room after two periods. Now the pressure is on North Jersey.

Badinoff adds a beauty early in the third to increase our lead to 5–3. Lyle Akouree gets one back for them, but an ENG by Libbet seals it. We win game 5 (6–4) and take three games to two lead in the best-of-seven series. We can wrap up this baby at home in game

6. We have to. None of us want to come back to North Jersey for a game 7.

Koontz Cup playoffs
AHA Eastern Division Semifinals Game
Sunday, May 4
Home versus North Jersey
Win 5–3; Charlestowne wins the series four games to two

This game sold out within minutes of us winning game 5 Friday night. Olympia Arena box office is selling standing room for game 6, although no such ticket exists on the manifest.

Essentially, we're telling fans, "Give me your twenty-five dollars for standing room and good luck finding a place to stand." What the hell? It could be the last home game in franchise history.

There is a buzz around the arena unlike anything I have seen in my sixteen seasons as an Icemen. The scalpers are out this morning for the pregame skate! Street vendors are set up at 11:00 a.m. There must be five hundred people milling around at lunchtime. The plaza in front of the arena already is taking on a party vibe.

Our room is quiet after warm-up. We know we have to win this one. We're fucked if we lose and have to go back to North Jersey for a game 7. Barnes can sense the tension, the pressure.

He has a speech ready, another motivational movie quote. He starts to address the room, then pauses. Barnes says, "I've got something I'd like to say to the team. But instead, I've got a better idea. Let's go right to the source. Let's go right to the man who actually spoke these memorable words."

Barnes steps aside and makes a sweeping gesture with his right arm. Out of the coach's office steps none other than Professor Charles Xavier himself, the founder and the leader of the X-Men.

In real life, this man is Hollywood legend, actor Patrick Stewart. He has a home in the Park Slope area of Brooklyn and is a close friend of Gotham Metros Coach Dave Haynesworth. Yoda gave his friend the backstory on the Icemen's last season, asked Stewart if he'd address the team before game 6.

Stewart steps into the center of the locker room and looks each player in the eye, slowly moving his head from left to right. He's in full X-Men mode now. Professor Charles Xavier speaks, "Since the dawn of existence, there have always been moments when the course of history shifted. Such a turning point is upon us now. There will be no going back. I do not know if victory is possible. I only know that great sacrifice will be required. And because the fate of many will depend on a few, we must make the last stand."

The boys explode. They are literally ready to run through a wall. Stewart exits to thunderous cheers and heads to the owner's box to watch the game. The Icemen leave the locker room three feet off the ground.

If our emotions are at a ten after Professor Xavier's motivation, we just take that up to eleven. Our owner sings the national anthem. That is followed by Zamboni driver, Donald MacDonald, standing in the Zamboni tunnel, swinging an effigy of a house painter complete with stained overalls, cap, and paintbrush. Our fans go insane.

House Painters have little chance after that. Our Professor, Crosby, does his best Magneto impersonation and draws pucks to their final resting place—his glove. Crosby wins his first playoff series as a pro. This Professor has lots of help from his D-Men. They block twenty-four shots, pucks that never get through to Crosby.

LeGault has the game winner, finishing off a sweet two-on-one with Karvaala. Hightower, Craigsen, and Cripenn get a goal each. I chip in with one goal and one assist. Icemen fans are delirious about this first-round upset. Biggest upset in AHA playoff history? Maybe.

No one can think of a bigger one off the top of their heads. A number 4 seed beating a number 1 that set records for wins and points in six games? Unheard of.

Our fans would have been completely satisfied if the season ended right there: first-round-playoff-series win over our archrival in the final season of the Icemen franchise. They all could die happy now. Icemen fans have zero expectations for round 2.

Players aren't looking ahead either. It's celebration time tonight! The Arena Lounge, Backcheck, and Richatelli's Sports Bar are all going off on a *Sunday night!* There will be a lot of people calling in sick to work Monday morning. None of the Icemen, however. Barnes gives everyone Monday off to recharge mentally and physically.

I have two VTs in the Arena Lounge before heading to the Backcheck. Their parking lot is packed. I park illegally between the trash dumpster and the back door. Tony isn't having anyone towed tonight. As I walk in, Crosby comes sailing past me on the shoulders of a group of Section 8 fans carrying him around the bar. The kid is just beaming. I spot Lee Harvey and Libbet in the corner and head that way. We didn't pay for a drink all night.

Tuesday, May 6

The hockey gods are smiling on the Icemen and on myself in particular. For round 2 of the AHA playoffs, the Eastern Conference Final, we'll play the Michigan Command. In their first-round matchup, Michigan beat Cleveland in seven games. Command finished number 2 in the East behind North Jersey. (Who dat?) Higher seed than us at number 4, so we'll open second round in Detroit Friday and Sunday nights.

Back to the Motor City. I'm in my last season as a Charlestowne Icemen with a chance to go to the Koontz Cup Final. It's a Hollywood tale. I wonder if Vince Vaughn will play me in the movie.

Our players would never throw shade and admit it publicly, but we like this matchup a *lot*. We won four of the six games against Michigan this season, going 2–1 both in their barn and at Olympia Arena. We outscored them 24–17 in those six games. We were just the opposite against Cleveland—only two wins in six games. Thank you, hockey gods.

Thursday, May 8

The night before game 1, I have dinner at Mom and Dad's. My brother and sister and their families make it as well. It's a treat to get everyone together, even if just for a couple of hours. It doesn't happen near enough.

Koontz Cup playoffs
AHA Eastern Division Final, Game 1
Friday, May 9 at Michigan
Win 4–2; Charlestowne leads the series one game to zero

This is a bad omen. Our game jerseys are missing.

We fly to Detroit instead of taking our normal bus ride. AHA rules dictate air travel for playoffs if trip is over five hundred miles. That's to make sure teams are in the host city in plenty of time for a playoff game. We hit the ground Thursday afternoon. Sal and Chuck haul the gear over to the arena before checking in at the hotel.

After this morning's pregame skate, they go to hang our game jerseys. The equipment bag with our road jerseys is nowhere to be found. Sal runs a bag check with the airline: sixty-four bags are scanned in at Charlestowne airport. Sixty-three bags are scanned out at Detroit Metro Airport. The bag with our road jerseys is lost somewhere in Detroit.

Chuck and Sal are in a full-blown panic. So are Barnes and I. We didn't pack our home jerseys for obvious reason. Those are back in Charlestowne hanging in the Icemen locker room waiting for game 3. We talk to AHA Commissioner Steve Archer. He will *not* allow us to wear Detroit's road jerseys. The colors for their two sets of jerseys are too similar. Archer feels it could cause issues during the whirl and speed of pro hockey, like checking your own teammate by mistake. Plus on the back are the names and numbers of the Command players.

It's now 4:00 p.m., three hours until puck drop for game 1. We need to somehow come up with a set of identical jerseys that are numbered (not enough time for nameplates), and the colors are different enough from the white Michigan home jerseys. We can't find a place in metro Detroit that can sell us eighteen matching jerseys and get them numbered and delivered to the arena by game time—not going to happen on this short notice.

The Command trainer hears about our predicament. He's been helping us since early afternoon, sourcing jerseys at retail, checking around the arena for the missing airline bag. He comes up with a possible solution. Not ideal but it might be our best option. He plays on an over-thirty-five men's league team and just finished washing their jerseys here at the arena. They are hanging and drying down near the home locker room.

There are eighteen matching jerseys, dark blue with white trim. The color contrasts nicely with Michigan's home whites, so check! Good to go there. The jerseys all have different white numbers, so check! These numbers won't match exactly the Icemen's real numbers, but at least we aren't stuck with three number 17 jerseys! We can live with that. I look at the front of the jerseys for the team name of this over-thirty-five men's league squad. There it is as big and bold as Charlie Sheen's liver: Corktown VD Clinic. Our best option for something to wear tonight for a round 2 AHA playoff game appears to be sponsored by a local STD doctor.

We have no choice. The first players arrive around 5:00 p.m. for a 7:00 p.m. game. As they enter the dressing room, it's obvious something is up: Those are *not* our road blues hanging in the stalls. The color of blue is way off. The numbers are weird. Sal tries to get them as close as possible. Half of the Icemen luck out. Their VD Clinic jersey has their real number on the back. Crosby has number 1, Hogaboom number 7, Badinoff number 8, Libbet number 14, etc. The other half of us are not so lucky. Hightower has number 21 instead of number 22, Slade has number 11 instead of number 12, Cripenn has number 26 and not number 29, and so on.

Our players are very confused. We don't give them any heads up about the jersey clusterfuck, just in case our real ones show up. No sense in getting the boys worked up about something we are hoping was going to get resolved, especially before a playoff game! As they hear the story about our lost equipment bag of road jerseys, the boys start to roll with the punches a bit more. The six starting defensemen come up with their own battle cry, "VD-D."

Guys like Hawkes, Crosby, and Slade could care less what the front of the jersey says. They're ready to go to battle. Hawkes keeps Michigan tough guy, Tim Robertson, in check all night. Looks like the story of the Toddfathers round 1, game 5 knockout of Hammer has made it to Detroit. Slade gets two goals and plays his usual no-quarter game on defense. He's always been a take-no-prisoners-and-shoot-the-wounded kind of guy. Crosby picks up from where he left off in round 1. We win game 1 in the Eastern conference final 4–2.

Heading back to the hotel on the bus, DeMarko is livid. No one tells him about the jersey snafu. He doesn't know until warm-ups that we are the Corktown VD Clinic for game 1. He is totally frustrated mostly because half the Icemen are wearing different numbers. Sometimes you can tell who a player is just by watching his skating style. Or what model helmet he wears. I guess DeMarko has a couple of our guys mixed up for most of the first period. I tell him, "That's the best thing about radio games. No one can tell if you're right or wrong. Just make it up."

DeMarko doesn't talk to me again until Saturday's practice and only to tell me he got laid after game 1.

Saturday, May 10

Our missing road jerseys show up. The story Sal is getting is dubious at best. The Command trainer brings the missing equipment bag to Sal after today's practice. He says the airport delivered it that morning. Airport allegedly told the Command trainer that the bag "fell off the conveyor at Metro airport baggage control and was out of site under the conveyer until an employee noticed it." Umm, yeah. I think the Command and their airport contact that helps them load bags for *their* road trips conspired on this one. Tried to take us off our game. To distract us. True or not, I start to spread that conspiracy theory. The boys are getting fired up about that—turn that anger into goal scoring!

Koontz Cup playoffs
AHA Eastern Division Final, Game 2
Sunday, May 11 at Michigan
Lose 5–1; series tied one game each

So much for the great jersey conspiracy. Crosby is shockingly bad. He sucks and gives up four goals in the first twenty-four minutes, less than a period and a half. Barnes yanks him after the fourth goal. Zeleski goes the rest of the way in a 5–1 loss.

More bad news. Pittinger is in for Richatelli, Pitt's first playoff game since round 1, game 4. He's happy to be back in the lineup and is working hard. Poor bastard can't get a break unless it's a bone. Pittinger takes a blazing slapper from Jimmy Akouree off his left foot in the second period. Pitt immediately hobbles to the bench and down the tunnel. Chuck gives us the news ten minutes later after the doctor checked DL. Pitt is out for the rest of the playoffs—broken left foot.

Koontz Cup playoffs
AHA Eastern Division Final, Game 3
Wednesday, May 14
Home versus Michigan
Win 3–2 in overtime; Charlestowne
leads the series two games to one

The pivotal game 3. Remember your AHA playoff history lesson from round 1. When a best-of-seven series is tied at one game each, the winner of game 3 goes on to win the series 69 percent of the time. Sixty-nine has always been my lucky number. It was in round 1. Let's hope it is again.

Crosby rallies. He's not great tonight but that thirty-six minutes he spent on the bench in game 2, watching Zeleski play was a good rest for him. It helps sometimes for a player to watch a game from the bench or press box without the pressure of playing. You see things from that perspective you may not while on the ice.

It's a really tight game. Michigan ties it 2–2 early in the third period on a power play goal by Jimmy Ballwagger. We carry the play in overtime, though, right from the start. Lee Harvey gets the kill shot in OT, beating Michigan goalie, Bill Perani, with a rising slap from top of the right face-off circle. Hightower *again* uses that oh-shit move where he fakes inside, goes outside and around the D, hits the after burner, and wires one. I congratulate him right after.

I say, "Sweet fucking goal! That move you make is killer! The fucking best ever!"

Lee Harvey says, "Well, it's not a fucking hobby." Fans go off into the warm, muggy Charlestowne May night completely happy. So do the Icemen.

Koontz Cup playoffs
AHA Eastern Division Final, Game 4
Friday, May 16
Home versus Michigan
Win 4–0; Charlestowne leads the series three games to one

Any overtime defeat is tough to shake off. It's magnified ten times when it's an OT playoff loss.

Two nights ago, Michigan badly wanted to steal game 3 in our building. They had some good scoring chances against Crosby but couldn't get that third goal past the rookie.

In game 4 tonight, Michigan gets *zero* goals on the Professor. Crosby makes a statement. He's a killer. He kicks out thirty-one of thirty-one shots. Playoff shutout in game 4. The boys stake Crosby by getting three goals in the first period. One would have been enough tonight.

Michigan had their heart ripped out in that game 3 overtime loss. Tonight in game 4, we essentially end their playoff life—two bullets in the back of their head.

It's a summer Friday night in Charlestowne. The Arena Lounge, Backcheck Lounge, and Richatelli's Sports Bar are usually packed anyway. Tonight, they're overflowed onto the patios and out into the streets. Icemen fans are celebrating a three to one series lead in round 2.

Saturday, May 17

AHA playoff history will tell you: Teams with three-games-to-one lead in a best-of-seven series *almost never* loses that series. Let's face it. That's true in any sport for any best of seven series. If you are up three games to one and only have to win one game out of the last three, nine times out of ten, you are going to be okay. But there is that 10 percent chance you *could* blow a three-games-to-one lead. Barnes and I are stressing to the team, "Let's end this Monday night and take TWO days off."

Olympia Arena bean counters, and our fans would love to see a game 6 back in Charlestowne.

But if you lose game 6 at home, you're on the road for game 7. Fuck that. Fuck the extra beer sales.

Like I said, let's end this Monday night at Michigan in game 5. Or to quote Evil Roy Slade, "Take no prisoners and shoot the wounded."

Sunday, May 18

Back in Detroit. Getting ready for game 5 tomorrow. My cell phone is blowing up—way too many ticket requests from family, friends, third cousins, Uncle Pete's bookie, Sharky from the old neighborhood, etc. When a guy you haven't talked to in twenty years is calling your cell, you know he'll be asking for free tickets. I'm going to have to put a crowbar in my wallet and buy some tickets for game 5.

Per AHA rules, each player gets four comp tickets per playoff game. So I start with four. Some of my teammates won't use any of their four freebies. The Europeans are usually good for extras.

The Western Canadians probably won't use all four. On the other hand, being in Detroit, our five Ontario natives will be looking for extra tickets too. The boys will give me all kinds of shit when I start asking for their tickets. "For fuck's sakes, Vito, don't be afraid to buy some tickets in your hometown. Then again, if you ever opened up your wallet, the sunlight would blind a bunch of presidents. Lincoln would be blinkin'." Or a favorite of Bradberry, "Spend some of that money, Vito. The Brink's truck doesn't follow the hearse." It doesn't? I'll have to speak to Stan Cappeletti about that.

Koontz Cup playoffs
AHA Eastern Division Final, Game 5
Monday, May 19 at Michigan
Win 6–3; Charlestowne wins the series four games to one

The boys listened. They want those two days off! We come out flying and get-first period goals from Bradberry and Craigsen. Crosby stops all eleven shots, and we lead 2–0 after one.

Michigan's Andy Davis cuts it to 2–1 early in the second. (Yup, that Andy Davis. I hit him so hard in the mouth earlier this season, I had two of his teeth embedded in my knuckles.) But before you can say *kaboom*, the Big Swede catches Robertson with his head down at center ice and separates him from the puck. Boomer headmans to Chrisler who feeds Hawkes and *bang*.

Hawkes beats Perani's high-blocker side, and we're back up by two goals. Five minutes later, Badinoff is bad enough. A sweet tip by Boris off a shot by LeGault skips past Perani. You can see the life go out of Michigan right then and there. They are done. Last person out, please turn off the lights. Slade is rubbing it in. Jimmy Ballwagger gets a very late goal for Michigan. No game impact at all. Slade makes pigeon coo-coo noises at Jimmy Ballwagger, mocking him for a garbage goal.

Final score is 6–3. We win the AHA Eastern Division Championship in five games. A quick series is huge right now. Two days off the ice, chance to heal up. Sit back and see who comes out of the Western Division Final, Musktown versus Texas. We hope they go seven games.

Commissioner Steve Archer is on the ice to present the Eastern Division Championship trophy to our captain, Reed Libbet. Libbet poses for a picture with the commish and trophy but won't touch the trophy. None of us will. Superstitions. Besides, that's not the trophy we want to win.

Let's hope Musktown wins the West. We had a better regular season record than they did. We'll get home ice advantage for the Koontz Cup Final if we face the Generals.

Thursday, May 22

First day back on the ice after clinching round 2. Boys are pumped! Musktown beat Texas last night, so we have home ice for the Koontz Cup final. The Marshalls took Musktown to seven games in the Western Conference Final. Generals had to play that much more playoff intensity hockey while we rested up. *Good*!

AHA office just released the game schedule for the Koontz Cup final, Charlestowne versus Musktown. I had to read it three times—must be a typo. We have home ice advantage, but instead of games 1 and 2 at home, schedule says game 1 in Charlestowne, game 2 in Musktown! What the fuck? Now who is trying to ass rape us in our final season? It turns out it was our good friends at Olympia Arena Management Company (OAMC). They can't even wait until this last season is over to bury us. Seven months ago, OAMC scheduled back-to-back Garth Brooks concerts for May 25 and 26. OAMC *never* thought for one second the Icemen might be playing May-June hockey. Garth Brooks' tour is locked and loaded. There would be no way to reschedule the concerts on three days' notice. If the arena pulls the plug on the shows now, there would be hell to pay: ticket refunds, sunk costs already associated with marketing and promoting two shows, etc. And the final determining factor: If the building yanked the show dates, Live Nation would put OAMC on their shit list for the rest of the year if not longer.

The players are berserk. We do get games 1, 3, and 4 at home, but still, the chance to get out on top of Musktown with two home wins is gone.

After our morning skate, I bump into Olympia Arena marketing head, Jimmy Bozatoni, in the service-level hallway. He walks right by me and doesn't even make eye contact, like I'm dead man walking. Bozatoni and his boss, GM Tony Mafasannti, hate us. They worked hard to get a new arena built without our hockey team as the anchor tenant. They still think that somehow, we purposely fucked up their Chinese gymnast national team promotion back in early January. And you know they were rooting for us to lose in round 2, so they wouldn't have to deal with this Garth Brooks clusterfuck.

Friday, May 23

Charlestowne commerce pretty much shut down at noon today, except for the bars! People go to lunch and never return to work. They are starting to gear up for game 1 of the final tomorrow night. The city is ready to party like it's the end of the world or the end of their hockey team.

Mayor Vizzyello declares today Charlestowne Icemen Day and encourages everyone to wear a jersey or team colors to work. What a joke. He's such a fucking phony. The guy that slit our throats on the new arena now wants to deliver the funeral eulogy. Fuck him. He won't even make the traditional friendly wager with the Musktown mayor. Mayor V wants nothing to do with this team. He sees this Koontz Cup Final series as more nuisance than notable. I hope Lynda Robinson gives him herpes.

Downtown is insane. Everyone is drinking and wearing Icemen swag. We snuck up on North Jersey in round 1, drew a favorable matchup in round 2, and *now* our fans expect us to win the whole damn thing. Their playoff attitude has gone from "Just happy to be here," to "How can they NOT win the cup in this final season?"

Koontz Cup Final, Game 1
Saturday, May 24
Home versus Musktown
Win 2–1; Charlestowne leads the series one game to zero

This is playoff hockey at its best. After our owner, Triple-R, sang the anthem, both teams play a tight checking game. We each have only a couple of scoring chances. Captain Libbet gets the game-winning goal, banging home a rebound right at the goal mouth. Pops also assists on our first goal scored by Slade. That's what captains do. They lead.

The other part of the game 1 leadership story belongs to the twenty-two-year-old rookie goalie from Warroad, Minnesota. Conner Crosby stands tall again, outdueling Musktown goalie, Robbie Kingfisher. I help the kid with a diving poke check on a Generals' breakaway. J.B. Scisson is the Musktown player I strip. He never gets a shot off. Scisson is a nineteen-year-old rookie. Early in my career, I played hockey with his dad, Earl. Damn, I'm (getting) old.

Fuck. I wish game 2 was in our barn, like it should be. We leave Sunday morning for Musktown.

Koontz Cup Final, Game 2
Monday, May 26 at Musktown
Lose 4–1; series tied at one game each

Fuck you, Garth Brooks and the horse you rode in on! Fuck you, OAMC! You're pissing on our graves already.

Fuck! I was afraid this would happen as soon as the Final schedule was released. This game should have been in Charlestowne, and we should be up two games to none. Instead, we give life to these cocksucker Generals. The boys are seriously pissed off at everyone.

We played okay and hung with the Generals for half the game. But Musktown parlays two power play goals with a four for four on the penalty kill to win.

Matt Wilsen's nose is fixed, best as can be. He is poking Steele all night trying to get him to go. Steele wouldn't take the bait. He shows great restraint for an insane rookie. Triple-6 does know this is a crucial playoff game, and he can't take a stupid penalty because Wilsen is chirping.

However, knowing and doing are two different things. We'll see how big Wilsen's balls are back in our barn for games 3 and 4.

Koontz Cup Final, Game 3
Thursday, May 29
Home versus Musktown
Win 5–2; Charlestowne leads the series two
games to one; the pivotal game 3

Back home, we play much better. This time, the Icemen have two power play goals (Hightower and Badinoff), LeGault has three assists, and Crosby is Crosby. That's a good formula for a win on most nights.

Game is out of reach late in the third when Steele and Wilsen have their rematch. The Olympia Arena crowd jumps to their feet when these two square off, anticipating another nose bite.

Not this time. Steele and Wilsen trade shots until they tire out. The linesmen separate them.

With less than five minutes to play in the third period, both head to their respective locker rooms. I'll give it to Steele on a decision, of course.

Koontz Cup Final, Game 4
Saturday, May 31
Home versus Musktown
Lose 3–2 in overtime; series tied at two games each

Oh boy, we fuck this one up. If we lose this series (*if*), we'll look back at this game. A bad line change in overtime costs us a home win. Instead of being up three games to one, we head back to Musktown for games 5 and 6 tied at two game each.

It ends quickly and without warning. Eight minutes left in overtime, Richatelli, getting only his second shift in the OT, is carrying the puck through the neutral zone. Libbet's line assumes (rightfully) that Tony is going to dump the puck in deep so we can change forward lines. Barnes is even yelling, "Change. Change." When they hear Barnes, Libbet's line peels off for the bench. Richatelli either doesn't hear Barnes or he freezes. Tony has the puck on his forehand cutting through center ice. Instead of dumping the puck in deep to get the line change, he slides it laterally to his right, expecting Hightower to be there. Lee Harvey is still headed to our bench. The new line has not jumped on yet. The puck hits the boards on the right side and ricochets right to Generals' defenseman, Jerry Sullivan. Richatelli is still going forward. Sullivan picks up the loose puck, skating in the opposite direction. He blows past Richatelli. Hogaboom is back and picks up Sullivan. But no one sees Tim Parker coming up fast behind Sullivan. Boomer stays with Sullivan who drives to net, then makes a perfect drop pass to Parker. Parker is a star, and he's paid like one. Parker gets the drop pass, uses Sullivan and Hogaboom as a screen, and whistles a one-timer past Crosby. The Professor is screened the whole way. He never saw the shot until it hits the back of the net.

We are crushed. The Icemen locker room is dead silent for fifteen minutes after the game. No one speaks. No one moves. We all sit there in our gear and stare at the floor, thinking about the one that got away. Richatelli, the townie from Charlestowne, has tears coming down his cheeks.

Our fans are almost as depressed as their Icemen. When Parker hammered the OT winner past Crosby, you could hear a rat fart. I'll bet half the building is still sitting out there, staring into their beers. They are thinking the same thing we are, *Woulda, coulda, shoulda.*

Koontz Cup Final, Game 5
Tuesday, June 3 at Musktown
Lose 3–0; Musktown leads series three games to two

Game 4 rattled our confidence. Game 5 crushed it. Musktown can smell it now. They dominate game 5 lead by goalie, Kingfisher. The Generals tender turns aside all twenty-three of our shots. Only one or two are good scoring chances. The funk from losing game 4 at home in overtime holds us back like a tequila hangover.

We are in serious trouble: down three games to two with game 6 in their barn Thursday night. The Icemen are facing possibly their last game in the thirty-eight years of the franchise. I don't sleep after this one. I don't want the grim reaper to take me any sooner than need be.

Wednesday, June 4

We're pulling out all the stops to keep the boys positive. Mr. Hockey visits before our morning skate. I announce his presence loudly to the room.

I say, "There he is! A living legend!"

Mr. Hockey jokingly says, "Not many of us left. And I'm not feeling all that well myself." He goes around the room, quietly saying a few words to each player. When Mr. Hockey is done making the rounds, he goes to the center of the locker room and addresses us as a group, "Let me leave you, men, with one last thought. You've been through a lot of playoff games in your careers. So have I. And the last time I checked, it was the first team to win four games that wins the series. It's not over." Mr. Hockey gives the room a thumbs-up. "Ferda," he declares.

Now it's Barnes's turn to motivate this group. He quotes Chuck Yeager. "You do what you can for as long as you can, and when you finally can't, you do the next best thing. You back up. But you don't give up." Barnes is getting really good at this. As soon as he's done quoting Yeager, a clip from the film *The Right Stuff* rolls on the big-screen TV in our locker room. It's the scene where Air Force test pilot, Yeager, while pushing the envelope as far as possible (chasing that demon), crashes the Lockheed NF-104A Starfighter test jet. Rescue crews race to the crash site. No one knows Yeager's fate. Did he eject safely? Did he eject and his parachute not work? Did he try to recover control of the F-104A but stayed inside too long and rode the test jet into the ground? Thick dark, black smoke is billowing up high on the horizon. Inside one of the rescue vehicles sits two men, including Yeager's longtime friend and jet test engineer, Colonel Jack Ridley. Both men are scanning the flat landscape, looking for any sign of Yeager. They race to the crash site.

The ambulance driver, pointing, says, "Sir. Over there. Is that a man?"

Colonel Ridley says, "You're goddamn right it is."

Cut to Yeager. Parachute balled up and under his left arm, helmet in his right hand. Face and neck blackened and burned from the crash and the smoke. Striding defiantly toward the rescue crews, he's not done and neither are the Icemen. We live to fight again.

Koontz Cup Final, Game 6
Thursday, June 5 at Musktown
Win 3–2; series tied at three games each

This is it. Time to walk the walk. We have to pull out game 6 on the road and force a game 7 back in Charlestowne. It's that simple.

The Generals come out hard. They want to close this out tonight. They do *not* want a game 7 back in our arena. Icemen go down 1–0 early, but before the first period ends, Budler gets that goal back. Craigsen puts us up 2–1 with a nifty deke on Kingfisher. Musktown's Greg Pursell ties it late in the second, and it stays that way. We go to the third period tied 2–2.

Everything comes down to the next twenty minutes—everything. I think about that during the second intermission. I'm thirty-nine and have been playing this game since I was five years old, the last sixteen years as a professional with the Charlestowne Icemen. And it all comes down to 1,200 seconds.

The existence of the Icemen. My career. I don't want it to end. Neither do any of the other seventeen men wearing the Icemen jersey. Both teams are tentative to start the third. After all, the next goal could win the series, the Cup. With 3:11 left in the third, staring at overtime, an unlikely hero emerges. Now I wouldn't say Brody Cripenn is the *last* Icemen I would expect to score the game-winning goal. But he'd be in my top three guesses! Offense is not his game. We picked up Cripenn from North Jersey in the Lufthammer trade because he is one of the best defensive forward in the AHA.

Craigsen, who is punching his ticket back to the Show with a great second half of this season, sets up the GWG. Craigsen carries the puck out of the far corner, looking for room to cut in front of the net for a shot. Both Generals defensemen and their center collapse on Craigsen.

They read the scouting reports. They know Craigsen is an NHL-quality offensive threat. They can't let him just walk right out in front. When they move to cut off Craigsen, Cripenn creeps in toward the Musktown goal from the opposite side. Craigsen flips a beautiful saucer pass over the stick of Generals' defenseman, Frank Waller, right onto the tape of Cripenn, who calmly flips a wrist shot under Kingfisher's right arm. Our bench explodes. Musktown fans get so quiet, I swear I can hear DeMarko screaming from the press box. We never look back. Crosby makes a couple of nice saves in the final three minutes and eleven seconds. Back to Charlestowne for game 7.

Friday, June 6

D-Day. After the morning skate, Barnes plays *Saving Private Ryan* for the boys. It's much deeper than a D-Day movie. It's about working as a unit, having each other's backs, overcoming adversity, and never giving up. The players watch intently, mostly in silence. The main message is getting through to them: You've got to earn it.

Koontz Cup Final, Game 7
Saturday, June 7
Home versus Musktown
Lose 4–3 in double overtime; Musktown wins
the Koontz Cup four games to three

Game 7s are a beautiful thing. Growing up playing pond hockey, it's what every little boy dreams about: scoring the game 7 winning goal in overtime. You raise your arms in triumph. Your teammates mob you. The fans are cheering and screaming your name. You make two laps around the arena holding the cup, which you present to your adoring fans.

That's the Hollywood ending, the feel-good ending. People love the hero. But they forget for every game-seven hero, there is the game-seven loser. It's true in any sport. Bill Mazeroski's ninth inning game 7 walk-off homer not only won the 1960 World Series for the Pirates, but for the rest of his life, Maz never bought another beer in Pittsburgh. Now the pitcher he took deep in game 7, Yankee Ralph

Terry, won 74 games for the Yanks over the next five seasons. But he's forever remembered for giving up that Game 7, bottom 9, walk off losing home run.

Same is true for hockey. Everyone remembers the Penguins beating the Red Wings in Joe Louis Arena in game 7 of the 2008–2009 Stanley Cup final. They remember the heroics of Pittsburgh goalie, Marc Andre Fleury, making twenty-four saves in that game-seven roadie. They forget how close Detroit came to winning back-to-back Stanley Cups. On the very last shift of the game with their goalie pulled, a rebound came loose to Nicklas Lidstrom at the left face-off circle. Lidstrom, a first-ballot hall of famer, arguably the best defensemen to ever play in the NHL (sorry, Bobby Orr fans), had the whole top half of the goal open. But he shot the puck low, and Fleury slid across to make a diving stop with two seconds remaining. Game. Set. Match. Cup.

Who will be the game-seven hero tonight? Who will wear the game 7 goat horns?

At first, it looks like the hero might be Icemen superstar Darren Hightower. We're losing 3–2 with fifty-one seconds left in the third period, less than one minute away from a game-seven loss at home. Cosby, the goalie, is pulled, and we have the extra attacker. Bradberry sifts a shot from the point through traffic. It hits Kingfisher halfway up his left pad and lands at his skates—huge scramble, bodies flying everywhere, and sticks slapping at the loose puck. Kingfisher makes two more point blank saves. Somehow out of the chaos, Lee Harvey, in his last game as an Icemen, knocks in a rebound to tie the game at three. We are headed to a game-seven overtime.

There is a buzz in the stands during the intermission before overtime the old arena has not seen in years, maybe ever—a constant din of noise punctuated by the occasional crescendo crash. Icemen fans think there is *no way* their team can lose game 7 at home, not after that late goal to tie it! It's the last game *ever* for the Icemen. They have to go out with the championship. To our fans, it is a foregone conclusion that we will win this game.

The boys are very quiet in the locker room, relishing the crowd noise, which is literally coming through the walls. We try and channel it into a positive. We know this is it—the last voyage. All aboard.

Just before we go out for overtime, Barnes paraphrases Herb Brooks's famous 1980 Olympics speech as the USA was about to hit the ice for the third period against the USSR.

Barnes says, "Last game of the season. Last game for the Icemen. Last game after thirty-eight years in Charlestowne. Last game for these fans. Last game for some of you. This is the moment you've worked for your whole lives. Since you were an eight-year-old mite. This is your time, not theirs. YOUR TIME."

Barnes, pausing for dramatic impact, says, "If you lose this game, you'll take it to your fucking graves."

Overtime starts out with both teams playing very cautious, not unexpected. After all, next goal wins the Cup. Very tight checking all around. Shots are only seven to five in the Icemen favor. Overtime is scoreless. Crosby makes a spectacular save on Tim Parker late in the OT. There are no power play chances. The referees have swallowed their whistles. You'd have to commit manslaughter to get penalized in a game-seven Overtime.

It's a Saturday night in Charlestowne. The Icemen are playing June hockey. Fans are dressed in shorts, tank tops, and flip-flops. It's game 7 of the Koontz Cup Final. It's the last game ever in the thirty-eight-year history of the Icemen franchise. And we are going to double overtime. Of course, Olympia Arena will break the law and keep beer sales open through the ten-minute mark of the second overtime.

Play goes back and forth in the second overtime. Each team gets a couple of long-distance shots on goal but nothing threatening until four minutes into the second OT.

It starts out as a very innocent-looking play. Icemen rookie defenseman, Damian Steele, carries the puck toward the opponent's end. Steele crosses center ice. As he goes to dump it in, the puck suddenly stops and stays at center ice. Puck is stuck there! Steele overskates the now-motionless puck. He has skated through an unseen water puddle on the ice. The puck stays in the puddle.

Musktown is quick on the transition and goes on the attack. One pass from their D at center ice (out of the puddle) to Tim Parker, charging down the left side. Parker is a stud, and we are all think he's going to shoot the puck. It's game 7 of the final. Double OT. Of course, Parker is going to shoot. Like Michael Jordan wouldn't take that shot. Same circumstances. You're fucking right he would. No way Air is dishing that off to Steve Kerr with the game (and championship) on the line.

Once he gets the zone, Parker winds up to fire the slapper. But then the unexpected. Parker fakes the shot and zips a pass across to his right wing to, of all people, Matt Wilsen! Wilsen is getting a rare shift in OT. Wilsen is a goon. In fact, he's the goon missing the tip of his nose after Steele chomped on it. His shooting skills: Wilsen couldn't hit the water if he fell out of a boat. But it's game 7, second overtime, and he hasn't played all that much. His legs are fresh compared to the other Generals. Musktown Coach Blumpkin is looking to give his wingers a forty-five-second blow. That's *the only* reason Wilsen is out there.

Wilsen catches Parker's pass cleanly, takes two more strides, then lets a slap shot go from thirty-five feet out. The puck is in slow motion. I swear I could jump off the bench, skate to that end of the ice, and knock it down out of midair. It's a fucking knuckleball! Connor has a bead on it, high-glove side, and is extending his left hand to catch the puck. Suddenly, it dips and hits the very bottom of Crosby's glove. The Professor can't squeeze it. Puck hits his wrist, then the ice, and trickles into the goal. Game over. Season over. Icemen over. We lose game 7 in double overtime 4–3. Official time of the game winning goal: four minutes and twenty seconds of the second OT.

Our fans are stunned. Many in the sellout crowd are sitting in stone-cold silence. Everyone is in shock including us. The Olympia Arena is silent, dead quiet except for the cheers of the Musktown Generals players and the couple of hundred of their fans who are lucky enough to get a game-seven ticket. A few half-full beer cups hit the ice as the officials skate off. No celebration for the home team and their fans. High above the ice, confetti and balloons stay fastened in nets, never to drop. Never ever again for the Icemen. The pyro and laser machines stay in the off position. No celebratory show tonight—canceled forever.

Back in our locker room, no one is talking. We are not looking at each other. We all stare despondently at the carpet. The Monte Cristo number 2 celebratory cigars I had ready for the boys stay in the humidor in my locker. Champagne that was on ice is quickly whisked out of the room through the trainer's entrance, so none of the players or coaches know it was even there.

After ten minutes of the most soul-crushing silence I have ever sat through, Barnes clears his throat and gets ready to speak. He talks about our character, our pride, how we had nothing to really play for in this final voyage of the Icemen, but yet we beat all the odds and made it game 7, double overtime of the Koontz Cup Final, creating memories along the way for our fans and for ourselves.

Barnes closes with the postgame speech by Coach Gary Gaines, Billy Bob Thornton's character from *Friday Night Lights*:

> Not a perfect ending. But being perfect is not about that scoreboard out there. It's not about winning. It's about you and your relationship with yourself, your family, your teammates and these fans. Being perfect is about being able to look the fans in the eye and know that you didn't let them down because you told them the truth. And that truth is you did everything you could. There wasn't one more thing you could've done. Can you live in that moment as best you can, with clear eyes, and love in your heart, with joy in your heart? If you can do that gentleman— you're perfect!

There aren't many clear eyes among the Icemen. Barnes is right. We did all we could. We left nothing in the tank.

Meanwhile, the Olympia Arena ice is well on the way to melting away forever. I find out weeks later that arena operations VP,

Vinnie Esposito, had turned off the ice chillers at the end of the third period. OAMC had stopped freezing the ice before the first overtime even started. By the time we hit the second overtime on a muggy June night in Charlestowne in an arena with antiquated air-conditioning, the melting ice was forming puddles. Vinnie Esposito better hope Damian Steele *never* finds out what caused that puddle on the ice in game 7, double OT. Steele will bite his whole fucking face off.

After sixteen seasons as an Icemen, for the last time in Charlestowne, I'm headed to the players' parking lot. I wonder to myself, *Which AHA teams might need a forty-year-old player coach?* I also start counting down the days until hockey training camps open in September. I can't wait.

CHAPTER 10

Where Are the Icemen? Ten Years Later

Goalie Conner Crosby	Perennial National Hockey League All-Star. Two-time Stanley Cup champ
Goalie Norm Zeleski	Goalie coach for a National Hockey League team
Defenseman Pat Bradberry	Successful online retailer in custom men's clothing
Defenseman Gerry Hogaboom	Head coach of Sweden Olympic women's hockey team
Defenseman J. F. LeGault	Somewhere in Quebec, smoking a cigarette, eating fromunda cheese, and drinking a Pepsi all at once
Defenseman Tom Pittinger	Owns a chain of sports medicine and orthopedic centers throughout Alberta and Saskatchewan
Defenseman Tony Richatelli	Took over Family Sports Bar in Charlestowne and franchised it along Eastern Seaboard—now with seventeen locations

Defenseman Jon Sanderson	Owns and operates Bro Surfing, retail outlets, Surf University, and summer youth camps. Also, the biggest cannabis retailer in British Columbia
Defenseman Damian Steele	Currently serving seven to ten years for aggravated assault in the Massachusetts Correctional Institute at Framingham
Forward Alexei Badinoff	Perennial National Hockey League All-Star on his way to five hundred career goals
Forward Da "Dale" Budler	Brigadier General in the Czech Republic Air Force
Forward Keeb Chrisler	Minister of the Department of Parks, Culture, and Sports, Province of Saskatchewan
Forward Duncan Craigsen	Got back to the Show. Current assistant coach for an NHL team
Forward Brody Cripenn	Still playing in the American Hockey Association
Forward Todd Hawkes	Cup of coffee in the NHL. Now Executive Director of the Nunavut Minor Hockey System
Forward Darren Hightower	Head coach of the University of Toronto men's hockey program
Forward Jeffrey Karvaala	General Manager and International Goodwill Ambassador for Christmas Land Resort and Casino, Lapland, Finland
Forward Reed Libbet	Assistant general manager with the NHL team that drafted him twenty years ago

Forward Bob Lufthammer	Ontario Region scout for NHL team
Forward Alfred Slade	Mayor of North Oaks, Minnesota
D/F Coach Vic "Vito" Barrzini	Wayne County sheriff in Detroit, Michigan
Head Coach Ken Barnes	General manager and head coach Gotham Metros. He has won two AHA Koontz Cup championships

American Hockey Association

Eastern Division	Western Division
Charlestowne Icemen	Elmdale Elmos
Cleveland Steamers	Great Lakes Storm
Gotham Metros	Highland Kilt Lifters
Michigan Command	Musktown Generals
North Jersey House Painters	Springfield Spirts
Old Market Lancers	Tech City Lazers
Peninsula Panthers	Texas Marshalls
Wilson Falls Driftwoods	Tri-City Thunderbirds

Goalies

#	Name	Nation	Hometown	Nicknames	HT	WT
1	Crosby, Conner	USA	Warroad Minnesota	Doc, Professor	6 foot-1	200
35	Zeleski, Norm	Canada	London Ontario	Z-man	5-foot-10	175

Defensemen

#	Name	Nation	Hometown	Nicknames	HT	WT
5	Bradberry, Pat	Canada	Dunrobin Ontario	Baron of Brown, King of Khaki	5-foot-11	190
7	Hogaboom, Gerry	Sweden	Stockholm Sweden	Boomer, Boom Town	6-foot-3	220
18	LeGault, JF	Canada	Sainte Foy Quebec	Frenchy, Smokey the Frog	6-foot-1	185
3	Pittinger, Tommy	Canada	Lloydminster Alberta	Whirlpool, DL	5-foot-11	195
2	Richatelli, Tony	USA	Charlestowne, SC	Townie, The Mayor	6-foot-0	180
16	Sanderson, Jon	Canada	Tofino British Columbia	Sandy, Machine	6-foot-1	205
6	Steele, Damian	USA	Fitchburg, Massachusetts	The Omen, Clark Kent, Triple 6	6-foot-2	210

Forwards

#	Name	Nation	Hometown	Nicknames	HT	WT
8	Badinoff, Alexi	Russia	Oblast Russia	Boris	6-foot-2	210
13	Barrzini, Victor	USA	Detroit Michigan	Vito, The Chairman	6-foot-0	195
20	Budler, Da	Czech	Prague Czech Republic	Buzz	5-foot-10	180
19	Chrisler, Keeb	Canada	Saskatoon Saskatchewan	Elf	5-foot-9	170
15	Craigsen, Duncan	Canada	Thunder Bay Ontatrio	Dunkie, Great White Hope	6-foot-0	195
29	Cripenn Brody	Canada	Cape Breton Nova Scotia		5-foot-10	180
25	Hawkes, Todd	Canada	Rankin Inlet Nunavut	One-Punch, Hawk, Chief	6-foot-2	215
22	Hightower, Darren	Canada	Toronto Ontatio	Lee Harvey, One shot one kill	6-foot-0	200
10	Karvaala, Jeffrey	Finland	Tornio Finland	Jeff	5-foot-10	180
14	Libbet, Reed	Canada	Stony Plain Alberta	Cap, Pops	6-foot-1	205
28	Lufthammer, Bob	Canada	Milton Ontario	Hammer	6-foot-4	235
12	Slade, Alfred	USA	North Oaks Minnesota	Evil Roy	6-foot-2	185

ABOUT THE AUTHOR

Steven Violetta has worked in the sports industry since 1986. His first nine seasons in the business were with three different minor league hockey teams, literally from coast to coast across the United States. With those teams, Steven performed every possible front-office work task except driving the Zamboni. Riding the buses with the players for nine years cemented his love for hockey and provided the inspiration for this fictional story. Since 1993, Steven has been a senior-level sports executive with several NHL and MLB organizations.

A native of Detroit, Michigan, Steven played travel amateur hockey through the midget age level and then club hockey in college. He's been working on the business side of sports teams ever since.